baking

100 BEST RECIPES

LESLEY MACKLEY

p

This is a Parragon Book
First published in 2003

Parragon
Queen Street House
4 Queen Street
Bath BA1 1HE
United Kingdom

Created and produced by
The Bridgewater Book Company Ltd,
Lewes, East Sussex

Photographer Ian Parsons
Home Economists Sara Hesketh & Richard Green

ISBN: 0-75259-936-4

Printed in China

NOTE

This book uses metric and imperial measurements. Follow the same units
of measurement throughout; do not mix metric and imperial. All spoon
measurements are level: teaspoons are assumed to be 5 ml and tablespoons
are assumed to be 15 ml. Unless otherwise stated, milk is assumed to be full fat,
eggs and individual fruits, such as bananas are medium, and pepper is
freshly ground black pepper.

The times given for each recipe are an approximate guide only because
the preparation times may differ according to the techniques used by
different people and the cooking times may vary as a result of the type of
oven used. Ovens should be preheated to the specified temperature. If using
a fan-assisted oven, check the manufacturer's instructions for adjusting the time
and temperature. The preparation times include chilling and marinating times,
where appropriate.

The nutritional information provided for each recipe is per serving or
per portion. Optional ingredients, variations or serving suggestions have
not been included in the calculations.

Recipes using raw or very lightly cooked eggs should be avoided
by infants, the elderly, pregnant women, convalescents and anyone
suffering from an illness.

contents

introduction

Baking is generally taken to mean the preparation of flour-based goods such as cakes, bread, pastry and biscuits, which are then cooked in an oven or, occasionally, on a griddle. The delicious, home-made food that results makes the effort in the kitchen worth while – particularly when it is served warm, straight from the oven. Baking also fills the kitchen with appetising aromas, and can be one of the most satisfying tasks, even for the reluctant cook!

The first ovens were wood-fired and were confined to relatively wealthy households. Poorer families baked on griddles or in Dutch ovens on top of a fire, or they might have sent the dough to a public bakehouse. Coal-fired ranges were developed in the nineteenth century, then gas and electric ovens were gradually introduced into modern kitchens in the twentieth century. Home baking was always a very important part of domestic life, but times have changed and the traditional weekly baking day is a thing of the past. Traditionally it was women who did the home baking, but nowadays most women work and do not have time to bake on a regular basis. Also, eating habits have changed and we have forgone the pleasures of afternoon tea and large meals ending with a pie or pudding. Most significantly, children no longer learn the traditional skills at school or in the kitchen at home.

However, there are signs that things are changing and we are rediscovering the art of baking as a pleasurable, satisfying and relaxing leisure activity. Modern equipment and ingredients, as well as a taste for less elaborate cakes and puddings, mean that anyone can produce delicious and impressive dishes with a minimum of effort.

electrical equipment

food processor: These have a multitude of uses, from mixing cake mixtures and pastry to kneading dough for bread, as well as chopping nuts and fruit, grating chocolate and puréeing fruit.

electric mixer: If you do a lot of baking, an electric mixer is invaluable. It can cope with large quantities and is better at creaming than a food processor. It is able to incorporate more air when whisking and can therefore be used for whisked cake mixtures and for beating egg whites for meringues. It will also fold ingredients such as nuts and fruit into a mixture without chopping them.

electric hand whisk: These are inexpensive and take the hard work out of creaming small quantities, whisking egg whites and whipping cream.

bread-making machine: These have recently become extremely popular. They mix, knead and bake the bread, but if you wish to shape your own bread, make rolls or buns or add extra ingredients before baking, you can still use the machine for mixing and kneading the dough.

measuring equipment

scales: When baking, it is important to measure the ingredients accurately. Reliable scales are essential and there are several types available. Electronic scales are the most accurate, particularly for weighing small quantities. They usually have a switch that allows you to select metric or imperial measurements, and you can set them back to zero after each addition when adding ingredients to a bowl, pan or jug. Traditional balance scales are sturdy and accurate, but it is not always easy to be precise when measuring very small quantities. Sets of weights

are available in either metric or imperial. Spring-balance scales are less hard-wearing and tend to be light, which makes them easy to knock over; if buying this type, choose one that has both metric and imperial measurements clearly marked.

measuring spoons and cups: Spoons are available in sets graduating from ⅛ teaspoon to 1 tablespoon. These are precise measurements; for example, 1 teaspoon = 5 ml. Measuring spoons should be used in preference to domestic spoons, which vary considerably in capacity. Unless otherwise stated, spoon measurements given in recipes are assumed to be level. If you also use American recipes, where all the ingredients are measured in cups, a set of measuring cups will be useful.

measuring jugs: A clear, heatproof jug showing both metric and imperial measurements is the best choice, because the measurements will be easy to read and the jug can be put in the microwave if you are heating milk or melting butter. It is a good idea to buy two jugs in different sizes – a small jug is essential for measuring small amounts of liquid, which tend to get lost at the bottom of a large jug.

bakeware

When buying any equipment, choose the best you can afford. This is especially true of cake tins, flan tins and baking trays. Cheap ones tend to be flimsy and can warp and buckle in the heat of the oven. Good-quality tins are solid and hard-wearing and conduct the heat evenly. Care should be taken when washing, drying and storing the tins. If the tins have a non-stick coating, it is important to wash them thoroughly in hot soapy water, otherwise a layer of grease will build up on the surface, rendering the coating less effective. Avoid using metal tools on a non-stick coating, as they will scratch the surface. It is important to dry traditional tins thoroughly after washing, to avoid rusting – it is a good idea to leave them in a cooling oven. Anodised aluminium is becoming popular and makes very good-quality, strong tins which will not rust and which conduct the heat well.

cake tins: Sandwich tins for sponge cakes should be bought in pairs, and 18-cm/7-inch and 20-cm/8-inch tins will be the most useful sizes. Deep round tins of the same diameters will be needed for fruit cakes. Like sandwich tins, they may have fixed or loose bases and may or may not have a non-stick coating. Deep square tins can be used instead of round tins for a variety of cakes, especially fruit cakes. Shallower square or rectangular tins are ideal for tray-bakes, brownies and layered pastries such as baklava. Springform tins with a metal clip that releases the sides are ideal for cheesecakes or any other cakes which may be particularly fragile or have a crumble topping that you will not want to invert. There are also a variety of ring moulds, kugelhopf tins and angel-food cake tins, which have a hole in the middle. They make attractive cakes, but an ordinary round tin can be made into a ring mould by placing a tin can in the centre. Some springform tins come with a variety of different bases, one of which will have a funnel in the middle.

loaf tins: Rectangular loaf tins are available in 450-g/1-lb and 900-g/2-lb sizes. Apart from their use in bread-making, they are ideal for teabreads and, in fact, almost any cake recipe can be baked in them when you want a loaf-shaped, easy-to-slice cake.

baking sheets and Swiss roll tins: Strong baking sheets are essential for biscuits, meringues, choux pastries and scones. Standing pies and tarts on a preheated baking sheet while baking will ensure that the pastry base will be crisp. They are usually completely flat with one raised edge, which makes it easy to slide off tarts and biscuits. It is a good idea to have two or three so that you can bake quantities of pastries and biscuits at one time. The most useful sizes are 20 x 30 cm/8 x 12 inches, 25 x 35 cm/10 x 14 inches and 28 x 40 cm/11 x 16 inches.

flan tins: Loose-bottomed tins with fluted sides are available in a wide range of sizes and depths. Those sold as tart tins are shallower than quiche tins. Professional cooks tend to use flan rings, which simply sit on a flat baking sheet. These can be either plain or fluted. Strictly speaking, fluted rings should be used for sweet tarts and plain rings for savoury flans and quiches.

patty tins: Six- and twelve-hole patty tins come in a variety of sizes. There are deep tins for large or mini muffins, and shallower ones for mince pies, tartlets, mini quiches and fairy cakes. In good cook shops, you will also find a variety of individual tart tins in a range of shapes for cocktail savouries.

additional equipment

There is no limit to the equipment that could accumulate in your kitchen cupboards and drawers, most of which might never be used, but there are some items that are essential for making your time in the kitchen as easy and efficient as possible.

cooling racks: It is important to place cakes and biscuits on wire racks to cool. This allows the air to circulate underneath, preventing the underside from becoming moist and heavy. If you make quantities of biscuits, you will need several of these.

sieve: This is necessary for sieving flour, icing sugar, cocoa, spices and baking powder. The sieving process not only removes any lumps, but it also helps to incorporate air, which will make the mixture lighter. A small sieve like a tea strainer is useful for dusting icing sugar or cocoa powder over a cake. Sieves are also used for straining custards before they are cooked or for removing solid flavourings such as orange peel or vanilla pods after infusing milk. For sieving fruit purées, you will need a stainless steel or nylon sieve.

mixing bowls: Choose large bowls, which allow you the space to incorporate plenty of air when creaming cake mixtures or whisking egg whites. Large bowls are also essential for bread-making, so that there is room for the dough to rise. China or glass bowls are preferable to plastic ones, as it is easier to ensure that they are spotlessly clean and greasefree, which is important when making meringue.

rolling pin: This should be at least 50 cm/20 inches long, made of wood, completely smooth and straight at the ends with no handles. A good rolling pin is essential for rolling out pastry and biscuits and, when oiled, is perfect for shaping tuiles and other curled biscuits.

cutters: A set of plain or fluted cutters in a variety of sizes is essential for cutting out pastry, biscuits and scones, and a few shaped cutters are also needed for biscuit making, particularly at Christmas or if you do baking with children. Cutters are either metal or plastic, and while plastic cutters are safer for children, metal ones cut more precisely, without dragging. This is especially important when using puff pastry, as it will not rise properly if it has not been cut neatly.

piping bags: Nylon piping bags are available in a range of sizes. They are strong and can be washed and reused. You will need a fairly large bag for piping cream, meringues, choux pastry and biscuit mixtures. For piping decorations you can make a small piping bag out of greaseproof paper, or simply snip a corner off a small polythene bag.

nozzles: A large plain and a large star nozzle are the most useful, for piping cream, meringues, choux pastry and biscuit mixtures. Smaller nozzles, with an adaptor to fit them into a piping bag, will be useful if you intend to do much in the way of cake decoration.

graters: Box graters with a variety of surfaces are the best. They are good for grating cheese, chocolate, citrus zest, ginger and nutmeg. Small graters are useful, especially for nutmeg – particularly the type that have a space in which to store the nutmeg.

pastry brushes: These are used for brushing milk or egg over pastry or scones, moistening the edge of pastry for pies, greasing tins or brushing a glaze over fruit. Flat brushes are the best for large surfaces while round ones are better for smaller areas. Choose good-quality brushes, as cheaper ones tend to shed their bristles as you brush. Wash them in hot soapy water and rinse well before drying them thoroughly.

tools: Wooden spoons should have long handles and rounded ends. They are ideal for beating, creaming and stirring in saucepans. A large metal spoon is essential for folding flour into cake mixtures and for folding in whisked egg whites. A long-handled, flexible rubber spatula will be needed for scraping mixture from the sides of a bowl. Flexible palette knives come in a range of sizes and are used for spreading fillings and icings or for lifting. A balloon whisk is ideal for whisking cream or egg whites or for stirring a sauce to prevent lumps forming. A long serrated knife is invaluable for slicing cakes into layers, and another very useful tool is a combination of serrated knife and spatula. A citrus zester is good for removing zest in delicate, thin strips. A swivel-bladed peeler is ideal for peeling fruit, removing strips of rind and making chocolate curls.

ingredients

Keep a selection of basic ingredients in the storecupboard so that you can bake a cake or rustle up a pudding whenever the mood takes you. Buy good-quality ingredients, and keep smaller amounts and replace them often rather than buying large quantities that quickly deteriorate. Store dry goods, such as flour, sugar, dried fruit and nuts, in a cool place in airtight containers.

flour: Flour provides the structure that holds the ingredients together, so it is important to choose the right kind. The way in which flours perform in cooking varies according to their ability to form gluten. Strong plain flour is high in gluten and is used in bread-making. It is also good for choux pastry.

Plain flour is used for pastry, most biscuits, rich fruit cakes and whisked sponges. It is also used in cakes that include whisked egg whites, as the air in the egg whites causes the mixture to rise. Plain flour can be made into self-raising flour by adding baking powder: generally, 4 teaspoons of baking powder to 450 g/1 lb flour. Wholemeal flour can be used instead of white flour in some cakes, but it gives a heavier texture and is often combined with white flour. After sifting wholemeal flour, add the bran that remains in the sieve.

Buckwheat flour is strong and dark and is traditionally used, combined with white flour, in blinis. Cornflour is a fine, starchy maize flour that gives a short texture to biscuits such as pastelitos. It is also added to the egg whites when making a pavlova or meringue roulade, to give the centre of the meringue a marshmallow-like texture. Polenta is usually combined with plain flour and gives a yellow colour and a crunchy, open texture to cakes, muffins and cornbread. Semolina is used in a similar way; it is fine-grained and rich in protein and starch. It gives a good open texture to Moroccan Orange & Almond Cake (see page 156), which allows it to absorb the warm syrup that is poured over after baking.

raising agents: Baking powder is a mixture of cream of tartar and bicarbonate of soda, which produces carbon dioxide, causing a mixture to rise. It starts to work as soon as it is added to liquid, which is why a cake mixture should be put in the oven as quickly as possible. When making a cake by the all-in-one method, you will add extra baking powder to the self-raising flour to help the cake to rise, because this method does not incorporate as much air as traditional creaming. Extra baking powder is also added to a scone dough. Sometimes bicarbonate of soda is used on its own to give heavy mixtures a lift, especially when the mixture has a spicy flavour, such as in Gingerbread People (see page 16). Yeast is used to make bread dough rise, as it produces carbon dioxide during proving. Purists may favour fresh yeast when baking bread, but the easy-blend dried yeasts are more widely available, are convenient to keep in a cupboard, are easy to use and produce excellent results.

sweeteners: Unrefined sugar is best for all baking and is used in most of the recipes in this book. It retains the sugar cane's natural molasses to give a smooth, mellow and rounded flavour. Caster sugar is used most frequently in these recipes. It is a fine-grained sugar with a subtle taste and it creams easily with butter and dissolves quickly when beaten with eggs. In both cases, caster sugar helps the mixture retain air. In melted cake mixtures, granulated or demerara sugar can be used because the sugar is dissolved in the early stages.

Some recipes use light or dark muscovado sugar. Both are soft and moist with a full rich flavour, but they tend to form into clumps in the packet and may need to be sieved before use. Icing sugar is a fine, powdery sugar for icing and buttercream fillings. It can also be used to sweeten pastry and makes a decorative topping when sieved over cakes and desserts. Unrefined icing sugar has

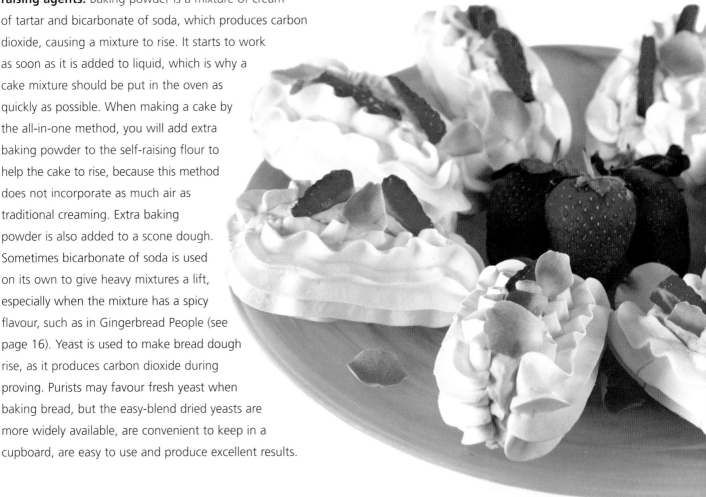

a golden colour, so refined icing sugar may be preferred when a pure white icing is required. Icing sugar should always be sieved before use. Some recipes use golden syrup, treacle, honey or maple syrup to add sweetness.

eggs: Unless otherwise stated, medium eggs are used in these recipes. For the best flavour, choose organic eggs. Eggs aerate a cake and provide richness and flavour. They will keep in the refrigerator for 1–2 weeks, but should be allowed to come to room temperature before use in order to achieve the best aeration. Alternatively, place the cold eggs into the mixing bowl and cover with warm water. By the time you have weighed all the other ingredients, the eggs will be at the right temperature and the bowl will be pleasantly warm for mixing the cake.

dairy produce and fats: Butter is used in most of the recipes in this book, as it gives the best flavour. However, if you prefer not to use butter, substitute a good-quality margarine. For all-in-one cake mixtures, choose a soft margarine that is especially for baking. Low-fat spreads are not a suitable alternative. Butter will keep in the refrigerator for 2–3 weeks, but it should be allowed to come to room temperature before rubbing in or creaming.

Where a recipe says 'butter, softened' it means that the butter has been out of the refrigerator for as long as it takes for it to become soft enough to cream easily. Use lightly salted butter for cakes, pastry and biscuits and unsalted for cake fillings and icings. Butter is used in shortcrust pastry to add flavour, but white cooking fat is usually added to make the pastry crisp.

Double cream is used in several of the recipes in this book. It contains a high percentage of fat, which enables it to be whipped firmly. Whipping cream is not a good substitute, as it does not hold its volume for as long as double cream.

Crème fraîche is included in the filling for the Peach Melba Meringue Roulade (see page 164), as its slight sourness is a good contrast to the sweetness of the meringue. Mascarpone is an Italian cream cheese that makes a rich filling for the Strawberry & Almond Roulade (see page 163). Cream cheese is an essential ingredient in the classic Manhattan Cheesecake (see page 160), and the soured cream that is also in this recipe is a foil to its richness. Buttermilk is a traditional ingredient in scones and its sourness helps them to rise.

nuts and fruit: Buy nuts in small quantities, as they become rancid and bitter after 3–4 months. Ground nuts lose their flavour even more quickly. If you buy unblanched almonds, they need to be blanched before use. Simply pour boiling water over them and leave for a few minutes; the brown skins will then slip off easily. To remove the brown skins from hazelnuts, heat them on a baking sheet in the oven, or in a dry frying pan, for a few minutes, then place them in a clean, dry tea towel and rub vigorously to remove the skins. Roasting nuts such as hazelnuts, almonds and pine kernels in a dry frying pan brings out their rich flavour, but it is easy to burn them, as they contain a lot of oil.

Freshly grated coconut adds moisture to cakes, and toasted coconut shavings make an attractive decoration. Dried fruits are used in many of the recipes in this book, and for decorating cakes. They should be stored in airtight containers, as they can dry out if not stored carefully. Most dried fruit, such as raisins and sultanas, will benefit from being plumped up by soaking overnight in orange juice, brandy or even hot water. Ready-to-eat dried fruits have already been soaked and are moist and soft. If you are using candied peel, it is always better to buy the pieces of fruit and chop them yourself rather than buy the pots of ready-chopped peel.

flavourings: If possible, it is always better to buy whole spices and grind them yourself, as they quickly lose their flavour once they have been ground. However, some spices, such as cinnamon, are difficult to grind at home. If you buy ready-ground spices, use them up quickly, and store them in a cupboard rather than on a work surface.

Vanilla pods should be sticky and pliable. Keep them in a jar of caster sugar and use the flavoured sugar when baking. As an alternative to vanilla pods, use liquid vanilla essence, which is made by macerating crushed vanilla pods in alcohol. Vanilla flavouring is a synthetic flavour and is not a good substitute. Orange flower and rosewater are strongly perfumed distilled flower essences that add an exotic flavour to cakes and syrups.

baking essentials

oven temperature: Oven temperatures vary so the recommended cooking times in recipes are guidelines only. The oven temperatures in this book are for a conventional oven. If you have a fan oven, consult the handbook, as the cooking times may be considerably shorter and the temperature may need to be reduced. It is important to preheat the oven before baking and for most purposes the oven shelf should be placed in the centre. In fan ovens the temperature is even throughout the oven, which is ideal for batch baking.

preparing cake tins: It is important to use the right size and shape of tin, though if you do not have quite the right size tin, it simply means that the cooking time will need adjusting. For instance, if the tin is slightly bigger than suggested in the recipe, the cake will be thinner and will cook more quickly.

It is worth taking time to prepare the tin before use to stop the cake from sticking. Unusually shaped tins need to be brushed with oil or melted butter and dusted with flour. Round, square or rectangular tins can be lined with silicone paper or greased greaseproof paper. To prevent rich fruit cakes from becoming too brown and drying out round the edges, secure a thick band of brown paper around the outside of the cake tin.

To line a round or square cake tin, brush the inside of the tin evenly with oil or melted butter. Cut a strip of paper, 5 cm/2 inches wider than the depth of the tin, to fit around the sides, overlapping slightly. Fold in one long edge of the paper by 2.5 cm/1 inch and crease well. Unfold and make cuts at 2.5-cm/1-inch intervals along the edge up to the crease. Place the paper strip in the tin so that the creased edge rests in the join at the base of the tin. Press into place on the greased sides and base of the tin. Place the tin on another sheet of paper and draw a pencil line round the base. Cut out the circle or square just inside the pencil line and lay the paper in the tin.

To line a small square or loaf tin, place the tin on a sheet of paper, large enough to extend up the sides and beyond them by 2.5 cm/1 inch. Draw a pencil line around the base and crease along the lines. From the longer edges, cut along the creases up to the marked lines. Grease the tin and line with the paper, tucking the flaps behind the longer sides.

For many recipes it is necessary only to grease and line the base of the tins with a paper circle or square. For loaf tins, line a greased tin with a strip of paper the width of the tin and long enough to extend up the short ends.

separating eggs: Carefully crack the shell on the edge of a clean bowl. Gently prise the shell apart in two halves, taking care not to split the yolk. Quickly pass the egg yolk from one half shell to the other, letting the white fall into the bowl below.

melting chocolate: Care must be taken when melting chocolate to make sure that it does not become overheated. The most reliable method is to put the chocolate in a bowl set over a saucepan of simmering water, making sure that the base of the bowl does not come into contact with the water. Remove the pan from the heat and leave until the chocolate has melted.

basic methods

cake-making: Many of the cakes in this book are made either by the creamed method or the all-in-one method. In creamed cakes, vigorous 'creaming' of the butter, sugar and eggs incorporates the air that is essential to produce a good cake. For best results, the ingredients should be at room temperature. First of all, beat the butter until soft and creamy, then add the sugar and beat until light and fluffy and doubled in volume. The beaten eggs are added a little at a time, beating well between each addition. If the mixture curdles, it will not hold as much air, so if it looks as if it might curdle, stir in a little of the flour. The flour should be folded in with a figure-of-eight movement with a large metal spoon. Do not stir or beat the mixture, otherwise the added air will be lost. The mixture should be smooth and creamy and drop reluctantly from a spoon. If it seems too stiff, add a little milk. The mixture may be creamed in a mixer, or in a bowl with a hand-mixer.

As the name of the method suggests, when making all-in-one cakes, all the ingredients are put in a bowl together and beaten until smooth. This is easy and quick if done in a food processor. Extra baking powder is added to compensate for the fact that this method does not incorporate as much air as the creaming method.

turning out and storing cakes: A cooked sponge will look well-risen and golden. The edge of the cake will be just beginning to shrink away from the sides of the tin. The cake should also feel springy when you press the centre lightly with your fingertips. A fine skewer inserted in the centre of the cake should come out clean and not sticky, though this is not a reliable test for cakes that contain fruit. Leave the cake to rest in the tin for a few minutes. If the sides of the tin are unlined, run a knife round the inside edge of the tin to loosen it. Turn the cake out on to a cooling rack and, if necessary, peel off the lining paper on the base. Leave to cool completely before decorating or storing.

To store undecorated cakes, wrap in greaseproof paper and foil, then store in an airtight container. To freeze, place the wrapped cake in a freezer bag, remove the air, then seal, label and date. Thaw, still wrapped, in a cool place. Cakes filled with cream or chocolate should be kept in an airtight plastic box in the refrigerator. Other layered cakes must be kept in a cool place.

pastry

It can be quite a time-consuming and skilful job to make flaky or filo pastry successfully, and because they are widely available in either the freezer or chiller cabinets in supermarkets, the recipes in this book use ready-made flaky and filo pastry. You can also buy good-quality, ready-made shortcrust and sweet shortcrust pastry, and they are very useful when time is short. However, they are not difficult to make, so some basic recipes are given on the page opposite.

When you are making pastry, make sure that you keep everything as cool as possible and try to avoid handling it more than necessary. For this reason, pastry made in a food processor is particularly successful. Follow the manufacturer's instructions for making pastry in a food processor. To make wholemeal pastry, replace half the white flour with wholemeal flour.

basic recipes

shortcrust pastry

makes: 1 x 15-cm/6-inch flan case
preparation time: 10 minutes,
plus 30 minutes chilling

115 g/4 oz plain flour
25 g/1 oz butter
25 g/1 oz white cooking fat
2 tbsp cold water

1 Sift the flour into a mixing bowl. Cut the butter and fat into small cubes and add them to the flour. Using your fingertips, gently rub the fats and flour together until the fat breaks down into tiny pieces and the mixture resembles fine breadcrumbs. This should be done as quickly and lightly as possible.

2 Stir in most of the water with a round-bladed knife. You may not need all the liquid, as the absorbency of flour varies. Alternatively, you may need to add a little extra liquid. Gather the dough into a ball and knead briefly. If it feels sticky, sprinkle over a little flour. Wrap the dough in clingfilm and leave to chill in the refrigerator for about 30 minutes.

sweet shortcrust pastry

makes: 1 x 20-cm/8-inch flan case
preparation time: 10 minutes,
plus 30 minutes chilling

225 g/8 oz plain flour
115 g/4 oz butter
15 g/½ oz white cooking fat
55 g/2 oz golden caster sugar
6 tbsp cold milk

Make in the same way as shortcrust pastry, stirring in the sugar after you have rubbed the butter and fat into the flour and using milk instead of water.

pâté sucrée

makes: 1 x 20-cm/8-inch flan case
preparation time: 10 minutes,
plus 30 minutes chilling

225 g/8 oz plain flour
115 g/4 oz butter, chilled and cubed
55 g/2 oz golden caster sugar
1 egg yolk
1 tsp vanilla essence
a little water

Make in the same way as shortcrust pastry, stirring in the sugar after you have rubbed the butter into the flour. Stir in the egg yolk and vanilla essence, with a little water if necessary, to make a smooth dough.

rolling out pastry: Sprinkle a little flour on a work surface and the rolling pin, then roll out the pastry, rolling away from you in one direction, using even pressure. Turn the pastry a quarter turn, anti-clockwise, occasionally. Do not pull or stretch the pastry.

to line a flan tin: Roll out the pastry until it is about 5 cm/2 inches larger than the flan tin all round. Use the rolling pin to help you lift the pastry over the tin. Lift the edges of the pastry so that it falls down into the tin. Press it gently, without stretching, against the edges of the tin.

Turn any surplus pastry outwards over the rim and roll the rolling pin over the top to cut off the surplus. If possible, chill for a further 30 minutes.

baking blind: Lightly prick the chilled pastry case, then line with a large sheet of greaseproof paper or foil. Fill with ceramic baking beans or dried pulses. Bake in a preheated oven at 200°C/400°F/Gas Mark 6 for 10–15 minutes, or until the pastry looks 'set'. Carefully remove the paper and baking beans and return to the oven for a further 5–10 minutes, or until the base is firm to the touch and light golden.

biscuits

There are many occasions when it is good to have a tin of home-made biscuits in the kitchen cupboard: when friends drop in for a chat, after school when hungry children need re-fuelling, to pop in lunch boxes, or just for those times when you fancy a little something with a cup of tea or coffee.

You do not need to be an experienced cook to be able to make successful biscuits and cookies, as they are surprisingly easy to make and require little, or no, special equipment. You can produce biscuits at home for a fraction of the cost of shop-bought ones, and not only do they cost less, they taste better too!

In this section you will find recipes for a whole variety of biscuits, from homely and chunky treats, such as Oatie Pecan Cookies (see page 20) or Double Chocolate Chip Cookies (see page 26), to light biscuits with delicate flavours, such as Lavender Biscuits (see page 31) or Pistachio & Cardamom Tuiles (see page 25), which are perfect for serving with ice cream. Children will enjoy making (and eating) Gingerbread People (see page 16) or Party Cookies (see page 18) and there are special biscuits such as Almond Biscotti (see page 24), which make an ideal accompaniment to after-dinner coffee. As well as sweet biscuits, there are recipes for savoury biscuits such as Spiced Cocktail Biscuits (see page 34) and Pesto Palmiers (see page 36), for serving with drinks.

gingerbread people

makes 20, using large cutters

prep: 30 mins, plus 30 mins cooling

cook: 15–20 mins

This is a favourite with children, who love to make the gingerbread shapes. The recipe makes a pliable dough that is easy to handle.

INGREDIENTS

115 g/4 oz butter, plus extra for greasing

450 g/1 lb plain flour, plus extra for dusting

2 tsp ground ginger

1 tsp mixed spice

2 tsp bicarbonate of soda

100 g/3½ oz golden syrup

115 g/4 oz light muscovado sugar

1 egg, beaten

TO DECORATE

currants

glacé cherries

85 g/3 oz icing sugar

3–4 tsp water

NUTRITIONAL INFORMATION

Calories	71
Protein	. . . . .1g
Carbohydrate	. . . . .13g
Sugars	. . . . .6g
Fat	. . . . .2g
Saturates	. . . . .1g

variation

The gingerbread dough can be cut into whatever shapes you prefer, so experiment with some creative ideas.

cook's tip

At Christmas, cut out star and bell shapes. When the biscuits come out of the oven, gently pierce a hole in each one with a skewer. Thread ribbons through and hang on the Christmas tree.

1 Preheat the oven to 160°C/325°F/Gas Mark 3, then grease 3 large baking sheets. Sift the flour, ginger, mixed spice and bicarbonate of soda into a large bowl. Place the butter, syrup and sugar in a saucepan over a low heat and stir until melted. Pour on to the dry ingredients and add the egg.

Mix together to make a dough. The dough will be sticky to begin with, but will become firmer as it cools.

2 On a lightly floured work surface, roll out the dough to about 3 mm/⅛ inch thick and stamp out gingerbread people shapes. Place on the prepared baking

sheets. Re-knead and re-roll the trimmings and cut out more shapes until the dough is used up. Decorate with currants for eyes and pieces of cherry for mouths. Bake in the oven for 15–20 minutes, or until firm and lightly browned.

3 Remove from the oven and leave to cool on

the baking sheets for a few minutes, then transfer to wire racks to cool completely. Mix the icing sugar with the water to a thick consistency. Place the icing in a small polythene bag and cut a tiny hole in one corner. Pipe buttons or clothes shapes on to the cooled biscuits.

party cookies

makes 16   **prep: 10 mins, plus 20 mins cooling**   **cook: 10–12 mins**

These cookies are studded with colourful sugar-coated chocolate beans, and are ideal for children's parties.

INGREDIENTS

115 g/4 oz butter, softened, plus extra for greasing
115 g/4 oz light muscovado sugar
1 tbsp golden syrup
½ tsp vanilla essence
175 g/6 oz self-raising flour
85 g/3 oz sugar-coated chocolate beans

NUTRITIONAL INFORMATION

Calories 146

Protein 1g

Carbohydrate 21g

Sugars 12g

Fat 7g

Saturates 4g

cook's tip

To make a slightly less sugary version of these cookies, you could use chocolate chips, cherries or chopped dried apricots instead of the chocolate beans.

1 Preheat the oven to 180°C/350°F/Gas Mark 4, then grease 2 baking sheets. Place the butter and sugar in a bowl and beat together with an electric whisk until light and fluffy, then beat in the syrup and vanilla essence.

2 Sift in half the flour and work it into the mixture. Stir in the chocolate beans and the remaining flour and work the dough together with your fingers.

3 Roll out the dough into 16 balls and place them on the prepared baking sheets, spaced well apart to allow for spreading. Do not flatten them. Bake in the preheated oven for 10–12 minutes, or until pale golden at the edges. Remove from the oven and leave to cool on the baking sheets for 2 minutes, then transfer to wire racks to cool completely.

nutty flapjacks

⏱ **cook: 20–25 mins**   ⏱ **prep: 10 mins, plus 30 mins cooling**   **makes 16**

These flapjacks are really quick and easy to make. They are perfect for adding to children's lunch boxes.

NUTRITIONAL INFORMATION	
Calories	.189
Protein	.3g
Carbohydrate	.19g
Sugars	.9g
Fat	.12g
Saturates	.4g

INGREDIENTS

115 g/4 oz butter, plus

extra for greasing

200 g/7 oz rolled oats

115 g/4 oz chopped hazelnuts

55 g/2 oz plain flour

2 tbsp golden syrup

85 g/3 oz light muscovado sugar

cook's tip

Be careful not to overcook the flapjack mixture, otherwise it will become hard and difficult to cut, rather than deliciously chewy.

1 Preheat the oven to 180°C/350°F/Gas Mark 4, then grease a 23-cm/9-inch square ovenproof dish or cake tin. Place the rolled oats, chopped hazelnuts and flour in a large mixing bowl and stir together.

2 Place the butter, syrup and sugar in a saucepan over a low heat and stir until melted. Pour on to the dry ingredients and mix well. Turn the mixture into the prepared ovenproof dish and smooth the surface with the back of a spoon.

3 Bake in the oven for 20–25 minutes, or until golden and firm to the touch. Mark into 16 pieces and leave to cool in the tin. When completely cold, cut through with a sharp knife and remove from the tin.

oatie pecan cookies

makes 15   **prep: 10 mins, plus 20 mins cooling**   **cook: 15 mins**

These light, crisp biscuits are delicious just as they are, but they also taste exceptionally good served with cheese.

INGREDIENTS

115 g/4 oz butter, softened, plus extra for greasing

85 g/3 oz light muscovado sugar

1 egg, beaten

55 g/2 oz pecan nuts, chopped

85 g/3 oz plain flour

½ tsp baking powder

55 g/2 oz rolled oats

NUTRITIONAL INFORMATION

Calories 143

Protein 2g

Carbohydrate 13g

Sugars 6g

Fat 10g

Saturates 5g

variation

For a slightly different taste, substitute other chopped nuts for the pecan nuts, such as walnuts or hazelnuts.

cook's tip

To save a lot of hard work, beat the butter and sugar together with an electric hand-mixer. Alternatively, use a food processor.

1 Preheat the oven to 180°C/350°F/Gas Mark 4, then grease 2 baking sheets. Place the butter and sugar in a bowl and beat until light and fluffy. Gradually beat in the egg, then stir in the nuts.

2 Sift the flour and baking powder into the mixture and add the oats. Stir together until well combined. Drop dessertspoonfuls of the mixture on to the prepared baking sheets, spaced well apart to allow for spreading.

3 Bake in the oven for 15 minutes, or until pale golden. Leave to cool on the baking sheets for 2 minutes, then transfer to wire racks to cool completely.

ginger-topped fingers

makes 16

prep: 15 mins, plus 30 mins cooling

cook: 40 mins

Shortbread fingers are always a satisfying treat, but a sticky ginger topping turns them into a real delight.

INGREDIENTS

175 g/6 oz butter, plus
extra for greasing

225 g/8 oz plain flour

1 tsp ground ginger

85 g/3 oz golden caster sugar

GINGER TOPPING

1 tbsp golden syrup

55 g/2 oz butter

2 tbsp icing sugar

1 tsp ground ginger

NUTRITIONAL INFORMATION

Calories 185

Protein 2g

Carbohydrate 19g

Sugars 8g

Fat 12g

Saturates 8g

variation

For decorative effect, pipe thin lines of white icing across the topping before it sets, then drag a cocktail stick across the lines.

cook's tip

The shortbread base will be quite soft when it first comes out of the oven, but it will become firm as it cools. These biscuits are best left to cool completely before serving.

1 Preheat the oven to 180°C/350°F/Gas Mark 4, then grease a 28 x 18-cm/11 x 7-inch oblong cake tin. Sift the flour and ginger into a bowl and stir in the sugar. Rub in the butter until the mixture begins to stick together.

2 Press the mixture into the prepared tin and smooth the top with a palette knife. Bake in the preheated oven for 40 minutes, or until very lightly browned.

3 To make the topping, place the syrup and butter in a small saucepan over a low heat and stir until

melted. Stir in the icing sugar and ginger. Remove the shortbread base from the oven and pour the topping over it while both are still hot. Leave to cool slightly in the tin, then cut into 16 fingers. Transfer to wire racks to cool completely.

almond biscotti

makes 20–24

prep: 20 mins, plus ⏲
20 mins cooling

cook: 25 mins ⏲

Biscotti are hard Italian biscuits that are traditionally served at the end of a meal for dipping into a sweet white wine, Vin Santo. They are equally delicious served with coffee or to accompany ice cream.

INGREDIENTS

250 g/9 oz plain flour, plus

extra for dusting

1 tsp baking powder

pinch of salt

150 g/5½ oz golden caster sugar

2 eggs, beaten

finely grated rind of 1 unwaxed orange

100 g/3½ oz whole blanched almonds,

lightly toasted

NUTRITIONAL INFORMATION

Calories	110
Protein	. . . . .3g
Carbohydrate	. . . . .18g
Sugars	. . . . .8g
Fat	. . . . .4g
Saturates	. . . . .1g

variation

As an alternative to almonds, use hazelnuts or a mixture of almonds and pistachio nuts.

1 Preheat the oven to 180°C/350°F/Gas Mark 4, then lightly dust a baking sheet with flour. Sift the flour, baking powder and salt into a bowl. Add the sugar, eggs and orange rind and mix to a dough. Knead in the toasted almonds.

2 Roll out the dough into a ball, cut in half and roll out each portion into a log about 4 cm/1½ inches in diameter. Place on the floured baking sheet and bake in the oven for 10 minutes. Remove from the oven and leave to cool for 5 minutes.

3 Using a serrated knife, cut the logs into 1-cm/½-inch thick diagonal slices. Arrange the slices on the baking sheet and return to the oven for 15 minutes, or until slightly golden. Transfer to a wire rack to cool and crispen.

pistachio & cardamon tuiles

 cook: 16–30 mins   prep: 15 mins, plus   makes 18
                           20 mins cooling

These wafer-thin, crisp, nutty biscuits are ideal for serving with fresh fruit desserts, or can be used as a delicious alternative to ordinary wafers for scooping up ice cream.

NUTRITIONAL INFORMATION

Calories 69

Protein 1g

Carbohydrate 10g

Sugars 7g

Fat 3g

Saturates 2g

INGREDIENTS

6 cardamom pods

55 g/2 oz butter, melted and cooled, plus extra for greasing

2 egg whites

115 g/4 oz golden caster sugar

55 g/2 oz plain flour

25 g/1 oz pistachio nuts, chopped

cook's tip

Do not be tempted to bake more than one tray of biscuits at a time, otherwise the second batch will become too firm before you have time to shape them.

1 Preheat the oven to 180°C/350°F/Gas Mark 4. Crush the cardamom pods and remove the husks. Grind the black seeds using a mortar and pestle and reserve. Grease 2 or 3 baking sheets and a rolling pin. Place the egg whites and caster sugar in a bowl. Whisk together with a fork until frothy.

2 Sift the flour into the bowl. Add the pistachio nuts and ground cardamom and mix with a fork. Add the butter and mix together thoroughly. Drop teaspoons of the mixture on to the prepared baking sheets, spaced well apart to allow for spreading. Using a palette knife, spread each one out slightly.

3 Bake in the preheated oven, 1 sheet at a time, for 8–10 minutes, or until the edges are firm. Lift the biscuits off carefully with a palette knife and place over the rolling pin while still warm. Leave to set for 1–2 minutes, then lift off carefully and transfer to a wire rack to cool. Store in an airtight tin.

double chocolate chip cookies

makes 24 **prep: 15 mins, plus 20 mins cooling** **cook: 10–15 mins**

These double chocolate biscuits, encapsulating pockets of melted chocolate chips, are a melt-in-the-mouth, mid-afternoon treat. They won't be in the biscuit tin for long!

INGREDIENTS

115 g/4 oz butter, softened, plus extra for greasing

55 g/2 oz golden granulated sugar

55 g/2 oz light muscovado sugar

1 egg, beaten

½ tsp vanilla essence

115 g/4 oz plain flour

2 tbsp cocoa powder

½ tsp bicarbonate of soda

115 g/4 oz milk chocolate chips

55 g/2 oz walnuts, roughly chopped

NUTRITIONAL INFORMATION

Calories 116

Protein 2g

Carbohydrate 12g

Sugars 8g

Fat 7g

Saturates 4g

---

variation

Use plain chocolate chips instead of milk chocolate chips, or substitute chopped pecan nuts for the walnuts.

---

cook's tip

The minimum cooking time will make cookies that are soft and chewy in the middle. The longer cooking time will produce crisper cookies.

1 Preheat the oven to 180°C/350°F/Gas Mark 4, then grease 3 baking sheets. Place the butter, granulated sugar and muscovado sugar in a bowl and beat until light and fluffy. Gradually beat in the egg and vanilla essence.

2 Sift the flour, cocoa and bicarbonate of soda into the mixture and stir in carefully. Stir in the chocolate chips and walnuts. Drop dessertspoonfuls of the mixture on to the prepared baking sheets, spaced well apart to allow for spreading.

3 Bake in the oven for 10–15 minutes, or until the mixture has spread and the cookies are beginning to feel firm. Leave to cool on the baking sheets for 2 minutes, then transfer to wire racks to cool completely.

easter biscuits

makes 24 **prep: 20 mins, plus 20 mins cooling** **cook: 10–15 mins**

In spite of their name, these biscuits are good to eat at any time of year! The mixed peel and currants give them a fruity, spicy taste, and a dusting of caster sugar makes them an especially sweet treat.

INGREDIENTS

175 g/6 oz butter, softened, plus extra for greasing

175 g/6 oz golden caster sugar

1 egg, beaten

2 tbsp milk

55 g/2 oz chopped mixed peel

115 g/4 oz currants

350 g/12 oz plain flour, plus extra for dusting

1 tsp mixed spice

GLAZE

1 egg white, lightly beaten

2 tbsp golden caster sugar

NUTRITIONAL INFORMATION

Calories 159

Protein 2g

Carbohydrate 25g

Sugars 14g

Fat 7g

Saturates 4g

variation

If you do not like mixed peel, you can substitute another 55 g/2 oz of extra currants instead.

cook's tip

Be careful when sprinkling the sugar over the glaze – any sugar sprinkled directly on to the baking sheet will burn on to its surface.

1 Preheat the oven to 180°C/350°F/Gas Mark 4, then grease 2 large baking sheets. Place the butter and sugar in a bowl and beat until light and fluffy. Gradually beat in the egg and milk. Stir in the mixed peel and currants, then sift in the flour and mixed spice. Mix together to make a firm dough. Knead lightly until smooth.

2 On a floured work surface, roll out the dough to 5 mm/¼ inch thick and use a 5-cm/2-inch round biscuit cutter to stamp out the biscuits. Re-roll the dough trimmings and stamp out more biscuits until the dough is used up. Place the biscuits on the prepared baking sheets and bake in the preheated oven for 10 minutes.

3 Remove from the oven to glaze. Brush with the egg white and sprinkle with the caster sugar, then return to the oven for a further 5 minutes, or until lightly browned. Leave to cool on the baking sheets for 2 minutes, then transfer to wire racks to cool completely.

mexican pastelitos

makes 40 **prep: 20 mins, plus 20 mins cooling** **cook: 30–40 mins**

These little South American-style biscuits melt in the mouth. They are traditionally served at Mexican weddings and are coated in icing sugar to reflect the white of the bride's dress.

INGREDIENTS

225 g/8 oz butter, softened, plus extra for greasing

55 g/2 oz golden caster sugar

225 g/8 oz plain flour

115 g/4 oz cornflour

1 tsp ground cinnamon

55 g/2 oz sifted icing sugar, to decorate

NUTRITIONAL INFORMATION

Calories 82

Protein 1g

Carbohydrate 10g

Sugars 3g

Fat 5g

Saturates 3g

cook's tip

These biscuits are traditionally made to this small size, but you could make larger biscuits, if you prefer.

1 Preheat the oven to 160°C/325°F/Gas Mark 3, then grease 2 baking sheets. Place the butter and caster sugar in a bowl and beat until light and fluffy. Sift the flour, cornflour and cinnamon into a separate bowl, then gradually work them into the creamed mixture with a wooden spoon. When well mixed, knead until smooth.

2 Take 1 teaspoon at a time of the mixture and roll into a ball. Place the little balls on the prepared baking sheets. Bake in the preheated oven for 30–40 minutes, or until pale golden.

3 Place the icing sugar in a shallow dish and toss the pastelitos in it while they are still warm. Leave to cool on wire racks.

lavender biscuits

cook: 12 mins

prep: 15 mins, plus 20 mins cooling

makes 12

Guests will be surprised and delighted by these original and unusual fragrant biscuits, which make the perfect accompaniment to a cup of tea in the afternoon.

NUTRITIONAL INFORMATION	
Calories	141
Protein	2g
Carbohydrate	17g
Sugars	6g
Fat	8g
Saturates	5g

INGREDIENTS

115 g/4 oz butter, softened, plus extra for greasing

55 g/2 oz golden caster sugar, plus extra for dusting

1 tsp chopped lavender leaves

finely grated rind of 1 lemon

175 g/6 oz plain flour

cook's tip

If you do not have a food processor, you can mix the dough by hand. Knead it into a ball before rolling out in Step 2.

1 Preheat the oven to 150°C/300°F/Gas Mark 2, then grease a large baking sheet. Place the caster sugar and lavender leaves in a food processor. Process until the lavender is very finely chopped, then add the butter and lemon rind and process until light and fluffy. Transfer to a large bowl. Sift in the flour and beat until the mixture forms a stiff dough.

2 Place the dough on a sheet of baking paper and place another sheet on top. Gently press down with a rolling pin and roll out to 3–5 mm/⅛–½ inch thick. Remove the top sheet of paper and stamp out circles from the dough using a 7-cm/2¾-inch round biscuit cutter. Re-knead and re-roll the dough trimmings and stamp out more biscuits.

3 Using a palette knife, carefully transfer the biscuits to the prepared baking sheet. Prick the biscuits with a fork and bake in the preheated oven for 12 minutes, or until pale brown. Leave to cool on the baking sheet for 2 minutes, then transfer to a wire rack to cool completely.

peanut butter cookies

makes 26 **prep: 20 mins, plus** ↺
20 mins cooling **cook: 12 mins** ⏱

These are easy biscuits for children to make. All of the ingredients are mixed together in one bowl, and the cookies themselves do not require any shaping or rolling out.

INGREDIENTS

115 g/4 oz butter, softened, plus
extra for greasing
115 g/4 oz crunchy peanut butter
115 g/4 oz golden caster sugar
115 g/4 oz light muscovado sugar
1 egg, beaten

½ tsp vanilla essence
85 g/3 oz plain flour
½ tsp bicarbonate of soda
½ tsp baking powder
pinch of salt
115 g/4 oz rolled oats

NUTRITIONAL INFORMATION

Calories 125

Protein 2g

Carbohydrate 15g

Sugars 10g

Fat 7g

Saturates 3g

variation

You can use smooth peanut butter rather than crunchy peanut butter, if you prefer.

cook's tip

When you flatten the cookies with a fork, make a slight impression on the surface with the tines of the fork to give them extra texture.

1 Preheat the oven to 180°C/350°F/Gas Mark 4, then grease 3 baking sheets. Place the butter and peanut butter in a bowl and beat together. Beat in the caster and muscovado sugars, then gradually beat in the egg and vanilla essence.

2 Sift the flour, bicarbonate of soda, baking powder and salt into the bowl and stir in the oats. Drop spoonfuls of the mixture on to the prepared baking sheets, spaced well apart to allow for spreading. Flatten slightly with a fork.

3 Bake in the preheated oven for 12 minutes, or until lightly browned. Leave to cool on the baking sheets for 2 minutes, then transfer to wire racks to cool completely.

spiced cocktail biscuits

makes about 20   **prep: 15 mins, plus** 🕐 **45 mins chilling (optional)**   **cook: 20 mins** 🕑

If you are looking for something a little different and original to help a dinner party go with a swing, these spicy biscuits are ideal for serving with pre-dinner drinks.

INGREDIENTS

115 g/4 oz butter, plus extra for greasing

140 g/5 oz plain flour, plus extra for dusting

2 tsp curry powder

85 g/3 oz grated Cheddar cheese

2 tsp poppy seeds

1 tsp black onion seeds

1 egg yolk

cumin seeds, for sprinkling

NUTRITIONAL INFORMATION

Calories	.88
Protein	.2g
Carbohydrate	.6g
Sugars	.0g
Fat	.7g
Saturates	.4g

variation

If you prefer, sprinkle with a little freshly ground cumin instead of the cumin seeds.

cook's tip

Chilling the dough and the rolled biscuits helps the biscuits to maintain their shape, but if you are short of time, it will not matter if you do not do so.

1 Preheat the oven to 190°C/375°F/Gas Mark 5, then grease 2 baking sheets. Sift the flour and curry powder into a bowl. Cut the butter into pieces and add to the flour. Rub in until the mixture resembles breadcrumbs, then stir in the cheese, poppy seeds and black onion seeds. Stir in the egg yolk and mix to a firm dough.

2 Wrap the dough in clingfilm and chill in the refrigerator for 30 minutes. On a floured work surface, roll out the dough to 3 mm/⅛ inch thick. Stamp out shapes with a cutter. Re-roll the trimmings and stamp out more biscuits until the dough is used up.

3 Place the biscuits on the prepared baking sheets and sprinkle with the cumin seeds. Leave to chill for a further 15 minutes. Bake in the preheated oven for 20 minutes, or until crisp and golden. Serve warm or transfer to wire racks to cool.

pesto palmiers

makes 20

prep: 10 mins, plus 20 mins chilling

cook: 10 mins

Serve these flaky and light palmiers to nibble with drinks, or as an accompaniment to a hearty, warming soup.

INGREDIENTS

butter, for greasing

plain flour, for dusting

250 g/9 oz ready-made puff pastry

3 tbsp green or red pesto

1 egg yolk, beaten with 1 tbsp water

25 g/1 oz freshly grated Parmesan cheese

NUTRITIONAL INFORMATION	
Calories	.70
Protein	.2g
Carbohydrate	.5g
Sugars	.0g
Fat	.5g
Saturates	.1g

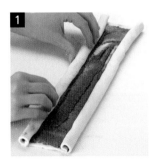

variation

As an alternative to the pesto filling, substitute Parma ham or chopped anchovy fillets.

1 Preheat the oven to 200°C/400°F/Gas Mark 6, then grease a baking sheet. On a floured work surface, roll out the pastry to a 35 x 15-cm/14 x 6-inch rectangle and trim the edges with a sharp knife. Spread the pesto evenly over the pastry. Roll up the ends tightly to meet in the middle of the pastry.

2 Wrap in clingfilm and chill in the refrigerator for 20 minutes, until firm, then remove from the refrigerator and unwrap. Brush with the beaten egg yolk on all sides. Cut across into 1-cm/½-inch thick slices. Place the slices on the prepared baking sheet.

3 Bake in the preheated oven for 10 minutes, or until crisp and golden. Remove from the oven and immediately sprinkle over the Parmesan cheese. Serve the palmiers warm or transfer to a wire rack and leave to cool to room temperature.

cheese & rosemary sables

⏱ **cook: 10 mins**   🕐 **prep: 15 mins, plus 30 mins chilling**   **makes 40**

The dough for these biscuits is made in a food processor, making these sables a quick and easy savoury treat.

NUTRITIONAL INFORMATION	
Calories	.80
Protein	.2g
Carbohydrate	.5g
Sugars	.0g
Fat	.6g
Saturates	.4g

INGREDIENTS

225 g/8 oz cold butter, diced, plus extra for greasing

250 g/9 oz plain flour

250 g/9 oz grated Gruyère cheese

½ tsp cayenne pepper

2 tsp finely chopped fresh rosemary leaves

1 egg yolk, beaten with 1 tbsp water

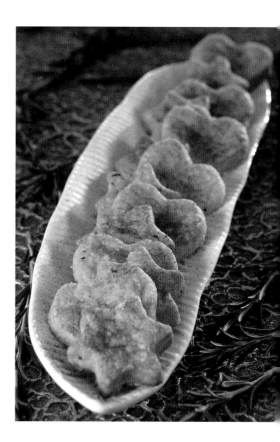

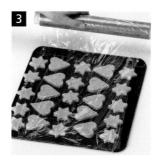

cook's tip

If you do not have a food processor, then place all the ingredients in a large mixing bowl and mix them together by hand.

1 Preheat the oven to 180°C/350°F/Gas Mark 4, then grease 2 baking sheets. Place the flour, butter, cheese, cayenne pepper and rosemary in a food processor. Pulse until the mixture forms a dough, adding a little cold water, if necessary, to bring the mixture together.

2 On a floured work surface, roll out the pastry to 5 mm/¼ inch thick. Stamp out shapes such as stars and hearts with 6-cm/2½-inch cutters.

3 Place the shapes on the prepared baking sheets, then cover with clingfilm and leave to chill in the refrigerator for 30 minutes, or until firm. Brush with the beaten egg yolk and bake in the oven for 10 minutes, or until golden brown. Leave to cool on the baking sheets for 2 minutes, then serve warm or transfer to wire racks to cool.

cheese straws

makes 24   20 mins, plus
30 mins chilling   cook: 10–15 mins

*Crisp cheese straws are irresistibly moreish. They make a wonderful
party food, and are popular with children and adults alike.*

INGREDIENTS

115 g/4 oz plain flour, plus extra
for dusting
pinch of salt
1 tsp curry powder
55 g/2 oz butter, plus
extra for greasing

55 g/2 oz grated Cheddar cheese
1 egg, beaten
poppy and cumin seeds,
for sprinkling

NUTRITIONAL INFORMATION

Calories 43

Protein 1g

Carbohydrate 4g

Sugars 0g

Fat 3g

Saturates 2g

variation

The same dough can be cut into
biscuit shapes rather than straws,
if you prefer.

cook's tip

Make sure that you mix the
dough thoroughly to prevent
any cracks in the dough
straws, otherwise they may
split apart while cooking.

1 Sift the flour, salt and
curry powder into a
bowl. Add the butter and rub
in until the mixture resembles
breadcrumbs. Add the cheese
and half the egg and mix to
form a dough. Wrap in
clingfilm and chill in the
refrigerator for 30 minutes.

2 Preheat the oven
to 200°C/400°F/Gas
Mark 6, then grease several
baking sheets. On a floured
work surface, roll out the
dough to 5 mm/¼ inch thick.
Cut into 7.5 x 1-cm/3 x ½-inch
strips. Pinch the strips lightly
along the sides and place on
the prepared baking sheets.

3 Brush the straws with
the remaining egg and
sprinkle half with poppy seeds
and half with cumin seeds.
Bake in the preheated oven
for 10–15 minutes, or until
golden. Transfer to wire racks
to cool.

bread, buns & teacakes

There are few cooking processes that are as satisfying as bread-making. It is not just the special flavour of home-made bread, or the mouthwatering aroma in the kitchen as it cooks, but there is something magical about seeing an unprepossessing lump of dough turning into a perfect loaf. When you taste your own bread, you will be taken back to those days when there was a family baker on every High Street.

If you think that bread-making is a difficult and lengthy process, the recipes in this section will convince you otherwise. With easy-blend yeast, it could not be easier to make yeast doughs and although it does take time for a dough to rise, you can be getting on with other things while that is happening.

A basic bread dough can be made into a base for hot Pepperoni Pizza (see page 42), and with the addition of a few other simple ingredients, can be transformed into a wide variety of delicious sweet and savoury loaves and buns, such as Cheese & Chive Plait (see page 45), Apricot & Walnut Bread (see page 56) or Chelsea Buns (see page 54). There are recipes for traditional festive breads, such as Stollen (see page 48) or Hot Cross Buns (see page 50). There are also recipes in this section for yeast-free teabreads, such as Date & Walnut Teabread (see page 61) or Banana & Chocolate Chip Loaf (see page 64), which are perfect for slicing and buttering for tea, and a classic Irish Soda Bread (see page 46) that takes minutes to make.

pepperoni pizza

serves 2   **prep: 20 mins, plus 30 mins rising**   **cook: 14–20 mins**

Pepperoni and tomato complement one another perfectly on this filling pizza. Dried red chillies give the topping quite a kick!

INGREDIENTS

PIZZA DOUGH

225 g/8 oz strong white bread flour, plus extra for dusting

2 tsp easy-blend dried yeast

1 tsp golden caster sugar

½ tsp salt

1 tbsp olive oil, plus extra for brushing

175 ml/6 fl oz tepid water

TOPPING

400 g/14 oz canned chopped tomatoes, drained

2 garlic cloves, crushed

1 tsp dried oregano

1–2 tsp dried chilli flakes

225 g/8 oz pepperoni, sliced

2 tbsp drained capers

225 g/8 oz mozzarella cheese, cut into thin slices

NUTRITIONAL INFORMATION

Calories 1154

Protein 65g

Carbohydrate 97g

Sugars 12g

Fat 59g

Saturates 25g

variation

If you would prefer a pizza with a little less heat, you can omit the chilli flakes from the topping.

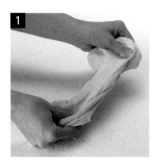

cook's tip

To save time, you can use a pizza dough mix, which can be found in any supermarket. These make a base which tastes warmer and crisper than ready-made versions.

1 Sift the flour into a warmed bowl. Stir in the yeast, sugar and salt and make a well in the centre. Stir the olive oil into the water, then stir into the flour. Mix to make a soft dough. Knead the dough on a lightly floured work surface for 5–10 minutes, or until it becomes smooth and elastic. Transfer the dough to a clean, warmed, oiled bowl and cover with clingfilm. Leave in a warm place for about 30 minutes, or until the dough has doubled in size.

2 Preheat the oven to 220°C/425°F/Gas Mark 7, then brush 2 baking sheets with oil. Turn the dough out on to a lightly floured work surface and knead lightly for 1 minute. Divide it in half and roll out each piece into a 25-cm/10-inch circle. Place on the prepared baking sheets.

3 To make the topping, place the drained tomatoes, garlic and oregano in a bowl and stir to mix. Spread half the mixture over each dough circle, leaving a margin around the edges.

4 Bake in the preheated oven for 7–10 minutes, or until the rim on each pizza is pale golden. Scatter the chilli flakes over the pizzas, then arrange the pepperoni slices and capers on top. Finally, place the mozzarella cheese slices on top. Return the pizzas to the oven for a further 7–10 minutes, then serve immediately.

black olive focaccia

serves 12 **prep: 20–25 mins,** ⏲ **plus 2 hrs rising** **cook: 30–35 mins** ⏲

Focaccia is an Italian flatbread made with olive oil. Try serving it with soups or salads, or on its own as an indulgent snack.

INGREDIENTS

500 g/1 lb 2 oz strong white bread
flour, plus extra for dusting

1 tsp salt

2 tsp easy-blend dried yeast

350 ml/12 fl oz tepid water

6 tbsp extra virgin olive oil, plus
extra for brushing

115 g/4 oz stoned black olives,
roughly chopped

1 tsp rock salt

NUTRITIONAL INFORMATION

Calories 200

Protein 5g

Carbohydrate 31g

Sugars 1g

Fat 7g

Saturates 1g

cook's tip

As the flavour of the olive oil is the most important part of this bread recipe, try to use a good-quality, well-flavoured olive oil.

1 Sift the flour and salt into a warmed bowl and stir in the yeast. Pour in the water and 2 tablespoons of the olive oil and mix to a soft dough. Knead the dough on a lightly floured work surface for 5–10 minutes, or until it becomes smooth and elastic. Transfer it to a clean, warmed, oiled bowl and cover with clingfilm. Leave in a warm place for about 1 hour, or until the dough has doubled in size.

2 Brush 2 baking sheets with oil. Punch the dough to knock out the air, then knead on a lightly floured work surface for 1 minute. Add the olives and knead until combined. Divide the dough in half and shape into 2 ovals about 28 x 23 cm/11 x 9 inches long, and place on the prepared baking sheets. Cover with oiled clingfilm and leave in a warm place for 1 hour, or until the dough is puffy.

3 Preheat the oven to 200°C/400°F/Gas Mark 6. Press your fingers into the dough to make dimples, drizzle over 2 tablespoons of oil and sprinkle with the rock salt. Bake in the preheated oven for 30–35 minutes, or until golden. Drizzle with the remaining olive oil and cover with a cloth, to give a soft crust. Slice each loaf into 6 pieces and serve warm.

cheese & chive plait

⏱ **cook: 35 mins**   ⏱ **prep: 30 mins, plus 1 hr 45 mins rising**   **serves 10**

This delicious, flavoured bread is ideal for serving with soup or as an accompaniment to a ploughman's lunch.

NUTRITIONAL INFORMATION	
Calories	.237
Protein	.9g
Carbohydrate	.35g
Sugars	.2g
Fat	.8g
Saturates	.4g

INGREDIENTS

450 g/1 lb strong white bread flour, plus extra for dusting

1 tsp salt

1 tsp caster sugar

1½ tsp easy-blend dried yeast

25 g/1 oz butter

115 g/4 oz coarsely grated Cheddar cheese

3 tbsp snipped fresh chives

4 spring onions, chopped

150 ml/5 fl oz tepid milk

175 ml/6 fl oz tepid water

vegetable oil, for brushing

beaten egg, to glaze

variation

This dough could be used to make small rolls instead of one large loaf.

1 Sift the flour and salt into a warmed bowl and stir in the sugar and yeast. Rub in the butter, then stir in the cheese, chives and spring onions. Make a well in the centre. Mix together the milk and water and pour into the well. Mix to make a soft dough. Turn the dough out on to a lightly floured work surface and knead for about 10 minutes, or until it is smooth and elastic.

2 Transfer the dough to a clean, oiled bowl and cover with clingfilm. Leave in a warm place for 1 hour, or until doubled in size. Preheat the oven to 220°C/425°F/Gas Mark 7, then brush a large baking sheet with oil. Turn the dough out on to a floured work surface and knead for 1 minute. Divide the dough into 3 pieces. Roll out each piece into a rope shape and plait the 3 pieces together, pinching the ends to seal.

3 Place on the prepared baking sheet and cover with oiled clingfilm. Leave in a warm place for 45 minutes, or until doubled in size. Brush with beaten egg and bake in the preheated oven for 20 minutes.

4 Reduce the oven temperature to 180°C/350°F/Gas Mark 4 and bake for a further 15 minutes, or until golden brown and the loaf sounds hollow when tapped on the bottom. Serve warm or cold.

irish soda bread

serves 12   **prep: 10 mins** ⏱   **cook: 35–40 mins** ⏱

Soda bread contains no yeast, so it is quick and easy to make – ideal when you're expecting guests for dinner.

INGREDIENTS

280 g/10 oz plain white flour, plus extra for dusting
280 g/10 oz wholemeal flour
1½ tsp bicarbonate of soda
1 tsp salt
1 tsp dark muscovado sugar
about 425 ml/15 fl oz buttermilk

NUTRITIONAL INFORMATION

Calories 167

Protein 6g

Carbohydrate 35g

Sugars 3g

Fat 1g

Saturates 0g

cook's tip

Buttermilk is usually available in most large supermarkets, but if you cannot find it, you can substitute ordinary milk instead.

1 Preheat the oven to 230°C/450°F/Gas Mark 8, then dust a baking sheet with flour. Sift the white flour, wholemeal flour, bicarbonate of soda and salt into a bowl and stir in the sugar. Make a well in the centre and pour in enough of the buttermilk to make a dough that is soft but not too wet and sticky. Add a little more buttermilk, if necessary.

2 Turn the dough out on to a floured work surface and knead very briefly into a large round 5 cm/2 inches thick. Dust lightly with flour and, using a sharp knife, mark the top of the loaf with a deep cross.

3 Place the loaf on the baking sheet and bake in the preheated oven for 15 minutes. Reduce the oven temperature to 200°C/400°F/ Gas Mark 6 and bake for a further 20–25 minutes, or until the loaf sounds hollow when tapped on the bottom. Transfer to a wire rack to cool, and eat while still warm.

chilli cheese cornbread

cook: 20 mins

prep: 10 mins, plus 20 mins cooling

serves 8

This golden yellow bread spiked with chillies was originally cooked over an open fire by pioneer settlers.

NUTRITIONAL INFORMATION

Calories 409

Protein 15g

Carbohydrate 43g

Sugars 3g

Fat 20g

Saturates 11g

INGREDIENTS

55 g/2 oz butter, melted, plus extra for greasing

115 g/4 oz self-raising flour

1 tbsp baking powder

1 tsp salt

225 g/8 oz fine polenta

150 g/5½ oz grated mature Cheddar cheese

2 eggs, beaten

300 ml/10 fl oz milk

1 fresh red chilli, deseeded and finely chopped

1 Preheat the oven to 200°C/400°F/Gas Mark 6. Grease a heavy 23-cm/9-inch cake tin or ovenproof frying pan and line the base with greaseproof paper. Sift the flour, baking powder and salt into a bowl, then stir in the polenta and 115 g/4 oz of the grated Cheddar cheese.

2 Pour the melted butter into a bowl and stir in the eggs and milk. Pour on to the dry ingredients, add the chilli, then mix quickly until just combined. Do not overmix.

3 Spoon the mixture into the prepared tin, scatter the remaining cheese on top and bake in the preheated oven for about 20 minutes, or until risen and golden. Leave to cool in the tin for 2 minutes, then turn out on to a wire rack to cool completely.

stollen

serves 10 | prep: 30 mins, plus 5 hrs rising | cook: 40 mins

Stollen is a delicious spiced Austrian fruit bread with a marzipan filling and is traditionally served at Christmas.

INGREDIENTS

85 g/3 oz currants	½ tsp ground nutmeg
55 g/2 oz raisins	½ tsp ground cinnamon
30 g/1⅛ oz chopped mixed peel	seeds from 3 cardamoms
55 g/2 oz glacé cherries, rinsed, dried and quartered	2 tsp easy-blend dried yeast
	finely grated rind of 1 lemon
2 tbsp rum	1 egg, beaten
55 g/2 oz butter	40 g/1½ oz flaked almonds
175 ml/6 fl oz milk	vegetable oil, for brushing
25 g/1 oz golden caster sugar	175 g/6 oz marzipan
375 g/13 oz strong white bread flour, plus extra for dusting	melted butter, for brushing
	sifted icing sugar, for dredging

NUTRITIONAL INFORMATION

Calories 360

Protein 8g

Carbohydrate 59g

Sugars 31g

Fat 11g

Saturates 4g

variation

You can substitute ground mixed spice for the nutmeg and cinnamon, and chopped no-soak dried apricots for the cherries, if you prefer.

cook's tip

An enriched dough such as this takes longer to rise than ordinary bread dough, so do not be tempted to put it somewhere hot to try to speed up the process.

1 Place the currants, raisins, peel and cherries in a bowl, stir in the rum and reserve. Place the butter, milk and sugar in a saucepan over a low heat and stir until the sugar dissolves and the butter melts. Cool until hand-hot. Sift the flour, nutmeg and cinnamon into a bowl. Crush the cardamom seeds and add them. Stir in the yeast. Make a well in the centre, stir in the milk mixture, lemon rind and egg and beat into a dough.

2 Turn the dough out on to a floured work surface. Knead for 5 minutes, adding more flour if necessary. Knead in the soaked fruit and the almonds. Transfer to a clean, oiled bowl. Cover with clingfilm and leave in a warm place for up to 3 hours, or until doubled in size. Turn out on to a floured surface, knead for 1–2 minutes, then roll out to a 25-cm/10-inch square.

3 Roll the marzipan into a sausage slightly shorter than the length of the dough. Place down the centre. Fold the dough over to cover the marzipan, overlapping it, and seal the ends. Place seam-side down on a greased baking sheet, cover with oiled clingfilm and leave in a warm place for up to 2 hours, or until doubled in size. Preheat the oven to 190°C/375°F/Gas Mark 5. Bake for 40 minutes, or until golden and hollow sounding when tapped. Brush with melted butter, dredge with icing sugar and cool on a wire rack.

hot cross buns

makes 12

prep: 35 mins, plus 2 hrs 45 mins rising

cook: 16–21 mins

There is nothing more tempting than the mouthwatering aroma of warm, spicy hot cross buns straight from the oven.

INGREDIENTS

500 g/1 lb 2 oz strong white bread flour, plus extra for dusting	75 g/2¾ oz butter, melted
½ tsp salt	1 egg
2 tsp ground mixed spice	225 ml/7½ fl oz tepid milk
1 tsp ground nutmeg	vegetable oil, for brushing
1 tsp ground cinnamon	
2 tsp easy-blend dried yeast	**CROSSES**
50 g/1¾ oz golden caster sugar	50 g/1¾ oz plain flour
finely grated rind of 1 lemon	25 g/1 oz butter, cut into pieces
175 g/6 oz currants	1 tbsp cold water
75 g/2¾ oz chopped mixed peel	
	GLAZE
	3 tbsp milk
	3 tbsp golden caster sugar

variation

If you would rather make mini hot cross buns, divide the dough into 24 pieces instead of 12.

cook's tip

Make sure that you press the pastry crosses gently but firmly on to the buns, so that they do not separate while they are baking.

1 Sift the flour, salt and spices into a bowl and stir in the yeast, sugar, lemon rind, currants and mixed peel. Make a well in the centre. In a separate bowl, mix the melted butter, egg and milk. Pour into the dry ingredients and mix to make a soft dough, adding more milk if necessary. Brush a bowl with oil. Turn the dough out on to a floured work surface and knead for 10 minutes, or until smooth and elastic. Place the dough in the oiled bowl, cover with clingfilm and leave in a warm place for 1¾–2 hours, or until doubled in size.

2 Turn out onto a floured work surface, knead for 1–2 minutes, then divide into 12 balls. Place on a greased baking sheet, flatten slightly, then cover with oiled clingfilm. Leave in a warm place for 45 minutes, or until doubled in size. Preheat the oven to 220°C/425°F/Gas Mark 7.

3 To make the crosses, sift the flour into a bowl and rub in the butter. Stir in the cold water to make a dough. Divide into 24 strips, 18 cm/7 inches long. To make the glaze, place the milk and sugar in a saucepan over a low heat and stir until the sugar has dissolved. Brush some of the glaze over the buns and lay the pastry strips on them to form crosses. Bake in the oven for 15–20 minutes, or until golden. Brush with the remaining glaze and return to the oven for 1 minute. Cool on a wire rack.

caraway kugelhopf

serves 8   **prep: 15 mins,** ⏲
plus 3–5 hrs rising   **cook: 30 mins** ⏲

Kugelhopf is a traditional German speciality that is a cross between a bread and a cake. The addition of caraway seeds to the recipe gives this kugelhopf an unusual flavour.

INGREDIENTS

225 g/8 oz strong white bread flour

55 g/2 oz golden caster sugar

2 tsp easy-blend dried yeast

4 tsp caraway seeds

50 ml/2 fl oz tepid water

115 g/4 oz butter, melted, plus extra for greasing

3 eggs, beaten

icing sugar, for dusting

butter, to serve

NUTRITIONAL INFORMATION

Calories	.267
Protein	.7g
Carbohydrate	.29g
Sugars	.8g
Fat	.15g
Saturates	.9g

cook's tip

Because a kugelhopf mould has a lot of detailed indentations, it is important to grease it thoroughly so that it turns out easily. If you do not have a kugelhopf mould, use an ordinary ring mould.

1 Sift the flour into a warmed bowl and stir in the sugar, yeast and caraway seeds. Make a well in the centre. In a separate bowl, mix the water with the butter and eggs. Pour into the dry ingredients. Beat until smooth. Cover the bowl with clingfilm and leave in a warm place for 2–3 hours, or until the mixture has doubled in size.

2 Grease a 20-cm/8-inch kugelhopf mould. Stir the mixture and turn into the mould. Cover with clingfilm and leave to rise again for 1–2 hours, or until doubled in size. Preheat the oven to 200°C/400°F/Gas Mark 6.

3 Remove the clingfilm and bake the kugelhopf in the preheated oven for

20 minutes. Reduce the oven temperature to 190°C/375°F/ Gas Mark 5 and bake for a further 10 minutes, or until well risen and golden brown. Leave to cool in the tin for 10 minutes, then turn out on to a wire rack to cool until warm. Dust with sifted icing sugar and serve immediately with butter.

orange & currant brioches

🕒 cook: 15 mins   🕐 prep: 30 mins,   makes 12
plus 2 hrs rising

Brioche is a light, rich French bread, which can be made as a loaf or buns. It is usually served with coffee for breakfast, but with the addition of raisins, it goes well served with butter for afternoon tea.

NUTRITIONAL INFORMATION	
Calories	129
Protein	4g
Carbohydrate	19g
Sugars	5g
Fat	5g
Saturates	3g

INGREDIENTS

55 g/2 oz butter, melted, plus
extra for greasing

225 g/8 oz strong white bread flour,
plus extra for dusting

½ tsp salt

2 tsp easy-blend dried yeast

1 tbsp golden caster sugar

55 g/2 oz raisins

grated rind of 1 orange

2 tbsp tepid water

2 eggs, beaten

vegetable oil, for brushing

1 beaten egg, to glaze

cook's tip

If you do not have brioche tins, you can use ordinary bun tins instead – the buns will not have patterned bases, but they will taste just as good.

1 Grease 12 individual brioche moulds. Sift the flour and salt into a warmed bowl and stir in the yeast, sugar, raisins and orange rind. Make a well in the centre. In a separate bowl, mix together the water, eggs and melted butter. Beat vigorously to make a soft dough. Turn out onto a lightly floured work surface and knead for 5 minutes, or until smooth and elastic. Brush a clean bowl with oil. Place the dough in the bowl, cover with clingfilm and leave in a warm place for 1 hour, or until doubled in size.

2 Turn out on to a floured work surface, knead lightly for 1 minute, then roll into a rope shape. Cut into 12 equal pieces. Shape three-quarters of each piece into a ball and place in the prepared tins. With a floured finger, press a hole in the centre of each. Shape the remaining pieces of dough into little plugs and press into the holes, flattening the top slightly.

3 Place the tins on a baking sheet, cover lightly with oiled clingfilm and leave in a warm place for 1 hour, until the dough comes almost to the top of the tins.

4 Preheat the oven to 220°C/425°F/Gas Mark 7. Brush the brioches with beaten egg and bake in the preheated oven for 15 minutes, or until golden brown. Serve warm with butter, if you like.

chelsea buns

makes 9   **prep: 30 mins, plus** 🕑 **1 hr 45 mins rising**   **cook: 30 mins** 🕑

Sweet and sticky Chelsea buns, with a hint of spice, are an irresistible addition to a traditional afternoon tea.

INGREDIENTS

25 g/1 oz butter, plus extra for greasing

225 g/8 oz strong white bread flour, plus extra for dusting

½ tsp salt

2 tsp easy-blend dried yeast

1 tsp golden caster sugar

125 ml/4 fl oz tepid milk

1 egg, beaten

vegetable oil, for brushing

85 g/3 oz icing sugar, to glaze

FILLING

55 g/2 oz light muscovado sugar

115 g/4 oz luxury mixed dried fruits

1 tsp ground mixed spice

55 g/2 oz butter, softened

NUTRITIONAL INFORMATION

Calories 266

Protein 5g

Carbohydrate 45g

Sugars 26g

Fat 9g

Saturates 5g

---

variation

For an extra spiciness, add ½ teaspoon ground cinnamon and ½ teaspoon freshly grated nutmeg to the filling.

cook's tip

When you place the buns in the prepared cake tin, place them close to each other in three rows, so that they join up into one single piece as they expand during cooking.

1 Grease an 18-cm/7-inch square cake tin. Sift the flour and salt into a warmed bowl, stir in the yeast and sugar and rub in the butter. Make a well in the centre. In a separate bowl, mix the milk and egg and pour into the dry ingredients. Beat to make a soft dough. Turn out on to a floured work surface and knead for 5–10 minutes, or until smooth. Brush a clean bowl with oil, place the dough in the bowl, cover with clingfilm and leave in a warm place for 1 hour, or until doubled in size.

2 Turn the dough out on to a floured surface and knead lightly for 1 minute. Roll out into a 30 x 23-cm/ 12 x 9-inch rectangle.

3 To make the filling, place the muscovado sugar, fruit and spice in a bowl and mix. Spread the dough with the softened butter and sprinkle the fruit mixture on top. Roll up from a long side, then cut into 9 pieces. Place in the prepared tin, cut-side up. Cover with oiled clingfilm and leave in a warm place for 45 minutes, or until well risen.

4 Preheat the oven to 190°C/375°F/Gas Mark 5. Bake the buns in the oven for 30 minutes, or until golden. Leave to cool in the tin for 10 minutes, then transfer, in one piece, to a wire rack to cool. Sift the icing sugar into a bowl and stir in enough water to make a thin glaze. Brush over the buns and leave to set. Pull the buns apart to serve.

apricot & walnut bread

serves 12   **prep: 25 mins,** ⏱   **cook: 30 mins** ⏱
plus 2–5 hrs rising

*Serve this fruit bread freshly made, sliced and buttered, or leave it
whole and invite guests to break off tasty morsels with their hands.*

INGREDIENTS

55 g/2 oz butter, plus   55 g/2 oz chopped walnuts

extra for greasing   150 ml/5 fl oz tepid milk

350 g/12 oz strong white bread   75 ml/2½ fl oz tepid water

flour, plus extra for dusting   1 egg, beaten

½ tsp salt   vegetable oil, for brushing

1 tsp golden caster sugar

2 tsp easy-blend dried yeast   TOPPING

115 g/4 oz chopped no-soak   85 g/3 oz icing sugar

dried apricots   walnut halves

variation

As an alternative to apricots, you
can substitute glacé cherries, dried
cranberries or dates.

cook's tip

Plaiting the bread in this way
makes it much easier to pull
the loaf apart into bite-sized
pieces after cooking. Leave the
loaf to cool before eating.

1 Grease and flour a
baking sheet. Sift the
flour and salt into a warmed
bowl and stir in the sugar and
yeast. Rub in the butter and
add the chopped apricots and
walnuts. Make a well in the
centre. In a separate bowl, mix
together the milk, water and
egg. Pour into the dry
ingredients and mix to a soft
dough. Turn out on to a

floured work surface and
knead for 10 minutes, or until
smooth. Brush a clean bowl
with oil, place the dough in
the bowl, cover with oiled
clingfilm and leave in a warm
place for 2–3 hours, or until
doubled in size.

2 Turn the dough out on
to a floured work
surface and knead lightly for

1 minute. Divide into 5 equal
pieces and roll each piece into
a rope 30 cm/12 inches long.
Plait 3 ropes together,
pinching the ends to seal, and
place on the prepared baking
sheet. Twist the remaining
2 ropes together and place on
top. Cover lightly with oiled
clingfilm and leave in a warm
place for 1–2 hours, or until
doubled in size.

3 Preheat the oven to
220°C/425°F/Gas Mark 7.
Bake the bread for 10 minutes,
reduce the heat to 190°C/
375°F/Gas Mark 5 and bake for
a further 20 minutes. Transfer
to a wire rack to cool. To make
the topping, sift the icing sugar
into a bowl, stir in enough
water to make a thin icing and
drizzle over the loaf. Decorate
with walnut halves and serve.

barm brack

cook: 1 hr

prep: 25 mins, plus 2 hrs 30 mins rising

serves 15

variation

Change your choice of dried fruit for different flavours, using currants and raisins on their own, or mixed with chopped dried apricots or even figs.

This Irish spiced bread was once traditionally baked with a wedding ring thrown into the mixture in the belief that whoever received the ring would be married within the year.

INGREDIENTS

650 g/1 lb 7 oz strong white bread flour, plus extra for dusting

1 tsp ground mixed spice

1 tsp salt

2 tsp easy-blend dried yeast

55 g/2 oz golden caster sugar

300 ml/10 fl oz tepid milk

150 ml/5 fl oz tepid water

vegetable oil, for brushing

55 g/2 oz butter, softened, plus extra for greasing

325 g/11½ oz mixed dried fruit

milk, for glazing

cook's tip

Allowing the bread to rise three times gives it its particular open texture, but if time is short, you can omit the second rising.

1 Sift the flour, mixed spice and salt into a warmed bowl, then stir in the yeast and 1 tablespoon of the caster sugar. Make a well in the centre and pour in the milk and water. Mix well, gradually incorporating the dry ingredients to make a sticky dough. Place on a lightly floured work surface and knead the dough until no longer sticky. Brush a clean, warmed bowl with oil, place the dough in the bowl, cover with clingfilm and leave in a warm place for 1 hour, or until doubled in size.

2 Turn the dough out on to a floured work surface and knead lightly for 1 minute. Add the butter and mixed fruit to the dough and work them in well. Return the dough to the bowl, replace the clingfilm and leave to rise for 30 minutes. Grease a 23-cm/9-inch round cake tin. Shape the dough into a neat round and fit in the tin. Cover and leave in a warm place until it has risen to the top of the tin. Preheat the oven to 200°C/400°F/Gas Mark 6.

3 Brush the top of the loaf lightly with milk and bake in the preheated oven for 15 minutes. Cover the loaf with foil, reduce the oven temperature to 180°C/350°F/ Gas Mark 4 and bake for 45 minutes, or until the bread is golden and sounds hollow when tapped on the bottom. Transfer to a wire rack to cool.

marbled chocolate & orange teabread

serves 12   **prep: 20 mins, plus** ⏲   **cook: 35–40 mins** ⏲
                        20 mins cooling

This recipe makes two cakes: one to eat straight away and one to freeze and keep for another day.

INGREDIENTS

150 g/5½ oz butter, softened, plus extra for greasing

75 g/2¾ oz plain chocolate, broken into pieces

250 g/9 oz golden caster sugar

5 large eggs, beaten

150 g/5½ oz plain flour

2 tsp baking powder

pinch of salt

grated rind of 2 oranges

NUTRITIONAL INFORMATION

Calories 286

Protein 5g

Carbohydrate 36g

Sugars 26g

Fat 15g

Saturates 9g

---

1 Preheat the oven to 180°C/350°F/Gas Mark 4. Grease and line the base and ends of 2 x 450-g/1-lb loaf tins. Place the chocolate in a bowl set over a saucepan of simmering water, making sure that the base of the bowl does not touch the water. Remove from the heat once the chocolate has melted.

2 Place the butter and sugar in a separate bowl and beat until light and fluffy. Gradually beat in the eggs. Sift the flour, baking powder and salt into the mixture and fold in.

3 Transfer one-third of the mixture to the melted chocolate and stir together. Stir the orange rind into the remaining mixture and place one-quarter of the mixture in each cake tin, spread in an even layer.

4 Drop spoonfuls of the chocolate mixture on top, dividing it between the 2 tins, but do not smooth it out. Divide the remaining orange mixture between the 2 tins, then, using a knife, gently swirl the top 2 layers together to give a marbled effect. Bake in the preheated oven for 35–40 minutes, or until a skewer inserted into the centre comes out clean. Leave to cool in the tins for 10 minutes, then turn out, peel off the lining paper and transfer to a wire rack to cool completely.

cook's tip

When you add the beaten eggs gradually in Step 2, the mixture may appear to curdle. Don't worry, this is perfectly normal.

date & walnut teabread

cook: 1 hr 5 mins– 1 hr 20 mins

prep: 20 mins, plus 20 mins cooling

serves 10

This moist and delightful teabread has sticky layers of sweet date purée running through it.

NUTRITIONAL INFORMATION

Calories	.396
Protein	.6g
Carbohydrate	.46g
Sugars	.35g
Fat	.22g
Saturates	.11g

INGREDIENTS

175 g/6 oz butter, plus extra
for greasing
225 g/8 oz stoned dates, chopped
into small pieces
grated rind and juice of 1 orange
50 ml/2 fl oz water
175 g/6 oz light muscovado sugar
3 eggs, beaten
85 g/3 oz wholemeal self-raising flour
85 g/3 oz white self-raising flour
55 g/2 oz chopped walnuts
8 walnut halves
orange zest, to decorate

cook's tip

Dates sold specifically for baking are often rolled in sugar; do not use these, as they will make the teabread taste too sweet.

1 Preheat the oven to 160°C/325°F/Gas Mark 3. Grease and line the base and ends of a 900-g/2-lb loaf tin. Place the dates in a saucepan with the orange rind and juice and water and cook over a medium heat for 5 minutes, stirring, or until it is a soft purée.

2 Place the butter and sugar in a bowl and beat together until light and fluffy. Gradually beat in the eggs, then sift in the flours and fold in with the chopped walnuts. Spread one-third of the mixture over the base of the prepared loaf tin and spread half the date purée over the top.

3 Repeat the layers, ending with the cake mixture. Arrange walnut halves on top. Bake in the oven for 1–1¼ hours, or until well risen and firm to the touch. Leave to cool in the tin for 10 minutes. Turn out, peel off the lining paper and transfer to a wire rack to cool. Decorate with orange zest and serve in slices.

spiced apple & apricot tea loaf

serves 10   **prep: 15 mins, plus 10 mins cooling**   **cook: 55–60 mins**

The firm texture of this cake makes it an ideal fruity snack for picnic hampers and children's lunch boxes.

INGREDIENTS

115 g/4 oz butter, softened, plus extra for greasing

140 g/5 oz light muscovado sugar

2 eggs, beaten

100 g/3½ oz no-soak dried apricots, chopped

2 eating apples, peeled and coarsely grated

2 tbsp milk

225 g/8 oz self-raising flour

1 tsp ground mixed spice

½ tsp ground cinnamon

NUTRITIONAL INFORMATION

Calories	258
Protein	. . . . .4g
Carbohydrate	. . . . .38g
Sugars	. . . . .21g
Fat	. . . . .11g
Saturates	. . . . .7g

cook's tip

No-soak dried apricots are sold in most large supermarkets as 'ready-to-eat' dried apricots, and are soft enough to chop very easily.

1 Preheat the oven to 180°C/350°F/Gas Mark 4. Grease and line the base and ends of a 900-g/2-lb loaf tin. Place the butter and sugar in a bowl and beat until light and fluffy, then gradually beat in the eggs.

2 Reserve 25 g/1 oz of the apricots, then fold the rest into the creamed mixture with the grated apples and milk. Sift in the flour, mixed spice and cinnamon and fold into the mixture.

3 Spoon into the prepared tin and sprinkle over the reserved apricots. Bake in the preheated oven for 55–60 minutes, or until risen and a skewer inserted into the centre comes out clean. Leave to cool in the tin for 10 minutes, then turn out and peel off the lining paper. Transfer to a wire rack to cool completely.

sticky ginger marmalade loaf

cook: 1 hr

prep: 10 mins, plus 10 mins cooling

serves 10

Ginger marmalade gives a wonderful warming flavour to this moist, sticky teabread, perfect with a cup of afternoon tea.

NUTRITIONAL INFORMATION	
Calories	.399
Protein	.5g
Carbohydrate	.45g
Sugars	.28g
Fat	.23g
Saturates	.11g

INGREDIENTS

175 g/6 oz butter, softened, plus

extra for greasing

125 g/4½ oz ginger marmalade

175 g/6 oz light muscovado sugar

3 eggs, beaten

225 g/8 oz self-raising flour

½ tsp baking powder

1 tsp ground ginger

100 g/3½ oz pecan nuts,

roughly chopped

cook's tip

If the marmalade loaf begins to brown too much before it has finished cooking, cover the top lightly with a piece of foil.

1 Preheat the oven to 180°C/350°F/Gas Mark 4. Grease and line the base and ends of a 900-g/2-lb loaf tin. Place 1 tablespoon of the ginger marmalade in a small saucepan and reserve. Place the remaining marmalade in a bowl with the butter, sugar and eggs.

2 Sift in the flour, baking powder and ground ginger and beat together until smooth. Stir in three-quarters of the nuts. Spoon the mixture into the prepared loaf tin and smooth the top. Sprinkle with the remaining nuts and bake in the preheated oven for 1 hour, or until well risen and a skewer inserted into the centre comes out clean.

3 Leave to cool in the tin for 10 minutes, then turn out and peel off the lining paper. Transfer to a wire rack to cool until warm. Set the saucepan of reserved marmalade over a low heat to warm, then brush over the loaf and serve in slices.

banana & chocolate chip loaf

serves 10   **prep: 25 mins, plus 30 mins cooling**   **cook: 1 hr 10 mins**

Bananas make this loaf cake beautifully moist, and combining them with chocolate makes this sweet bread a favourite with children.

INGREDIENTS

115 g/4 oz butter, softened, plus extra for greasing

175 g/6 oz plain flour

1 tsp bicarbonate of soda

pinch of salt

1 tsp ground cinnamon

175 g/6 oz golden caster sugar

2 large ripe bananas, mashed

2 eggs, beaten

5 tbsp boiling water

175 g/6 oz plain chocolate chips

TO SERVE

whipped cream

ready-made chocolate decorations

NUTRITIONAL INFORMATION

Calories 344

Protein 4g

Carbohydrate 49g

Sugars 34g

Fat 16g

Saturates 10g

variation

Substituting milk chocolate chips for the plain chips will give the loaf a slightly richer taste.

cook's tip

Because this is a very moist cake, it is not possible to test with a skewer, which will always come out sticky.

1 Preheat the oven to 160°C/325°F/Gas Mark 3. Grease and line the base and sides of a 900-g/2-lb loaf tin. Sift the flour, bicarbonate of soda, salt and cinnamon into a bowl and reserve. Place the butter and sugar in a bowl and beat together until light and fluffy.

2 Beat in the bananas and then the eggs. The mixture may look curdled, but this is perfectly normal. Stir in the flour mixture alternately with the boiling water until just combined, then stir in the chocolate chips.

3 Spoon into the prepared tin and smooth the top. Bake in the preheated oven for 1 hour 10 minutes, or until well risen, golden brown and firm to the touch. Leave to cool in the tin for 30 minutes, then turn out and peel off the lining paper. Transfer to a wire rack to cool completely, then serve in slices with a little whipped cream decorated with chocolate decorations.

glossy fruit loaf

🕛 **cook: 1 hr 30 mins–
1 hr 45 mins**

🕛 **prep: 20 mins, plus 8 hrs
20 mins soaking/cooling**

serves 10

NUTRITIONAL INFORMATION
Calories 400
Protein 6g
Carbohydrate 53g
Sugars 39g
Fat 20g
Saturates 9g

*This is a rich, sweet fruit loaf, ideal for family celebrations
or parties, and tastes superb with a cup of hot tea.*

variation

Try using several different types of
dried fruit and nuts, according to your
personal taste.

INGREDIENTS

55 g/2 oz raisins

85 g/3 oz no-soak dried apricots,
roughly chopped

55 g/2 oz stoned dates, chopped

90 ml/3¼ fl oz cold black tea

115 g/4 oz butter, plus extra
for greasing

115 g/4 oz light muscovado sugar

2 eggs, beaten

175 g/6 oz self-raising flour, sifted

55 g/2 oz glacé pineapple,
roughly chopped

85 g/3 oz glacé cherries, halved

85 g/3 oz Brazil nuts, roughly chopped

TOPPING

25 g/1 oz walnut halves

25 g/1 oz Brazil nuts

55 g/2 oz glacé cherries, halved

2 tbsp apricot jam, sieved

cook's tip

Soaking dried fruit in cold
black tea makes the fruit
plump and juicy, which
gives fruitbread an extra
flavour and moistness.

1 Place the raisins,
apricots and dates in a
bowl, pour over the tea, cover
and leave to soak for 8 hours,
or overnight. Preheat the oven
to 160°C/325°F/Gas Mark 3.
Grease and line the base and
ends of a 900-g/2-lb loaf tin.
Place the butter and sugar in
a bowl and beat together until
light and fluffy.

2 Gradually beat in the
eggs, then fold in
the flour alternately with the
soaked fruit. Gently stir in
the pineapple, cherries and
chopped nuts. Turn the
mixture into the prepared tin.
To make the topping, arrange
the walnuts, Brazil nuts and
cherries on top.

3 Bake in the preheated
oven for 1½–1¾ hours,
or until a skewer inserted into
the centre comes out clean.
Leave to cool in the tin for
10 minutes, then turn out
and peel off the lining paper.
Transfer to a wire rack to cool
completely. Warm the apricot
jam and brush over the top of
the cake.

pies, tarts & pastries

At the beginning of this book are recipes for basic pastries that are simple to make, especially if you use a food processor. However, if you are nervous about making pastry, there is no need to avoid baking the recipes in this section, as it is easy to buy excellent ready-made pastries. When it comes to puff pastry or filo pastry, most people will be happy to use the ready-prepared varieties.

In this section, you will find recipes from all over the world, such as a fresh and light Sicilian Ricotta Tart (see page 89), America's favourite Pecan Pie (see page 72) and a gloriously sticky Baklava (see page 80) from Greece. Some of the easiest recipes are those made with filo pastry, such as Pear & Pecan Strudel (see page 88), where the pastry is simply rolled round a filling, without the need for rolling out or lining tart tins. There are recipes for every occasion, such as a Treacle & Orange Tart (see page 79) or Coconut Tart (see page 70) for a family lunch, and fashionable Tarte au Citron (see page 76) or a rich Chocolate, Chestnut & Ginger Tart (see page 90) for a dinner party. Individual tarts and pastries look very attractive served as a dessert and are also perfect for serving with afternoon tea. Summer Fruit Tartlets (see page 86) or Raspberry Eclairs (see page 84) would be ideal for a summer tea in the garden. There are also recipes for savoury pastries, which are ideal for serving in a variety of ways. Crab & Ginger Triangles (see page 94) are a delicious accompaniment to drinks, Filo Tarts with Avocado Salsa (see page 95) and Mini Choux Puffs with Prawn Cocktail (see page 96) are an ideal starter, and Greek Feta & Olive Tarts (see page 98) make a quick and easy lunch served with salad.

coconut tart

serves 8

prep: 25 mins, plus 1 hr cooling

cook: 55 mins

Coconut makes the filling in this tart lovely and moist. Serve it as a refreshing end to a heavy main meal.

INGREDIENTS

butter, for greasing

plain flour, for dusting

1 quantity Sweet Shortcrust Pastry

(see page 13)

FILLING

2 eggs

grated rind and juice of 2 lemons

200 g/7 oz golden caster sugar

375 ml/13 fl oz double cream

250 g/9 oz desiccated coconut

NUTRITIONAL INFORMATION

Calories 772

Protein 7g

Carbohydrate 59g

Sugars 38g

Fat 58g

Saturates 40g

---

variation

Add ½ teaspoon of nutmeg to the filling mixture to give the tart a little extra flavour, if you like.

---

cook's tip

This coconut tart tastes exceptionally good if you serve it accompanied by a fresh passion fruit purée. Desiccated coconut is usually available in large supermarkets.

1 Preheat the oven to 200°C/400°F/Gas Mark 6, then grease a 23-cm/ 9-inch tart tin. On a lightly floured work surface, roll out the pastry and use it to line the prepared tin, then bake blind (see page 13). Reduce the oven temperature to160°C/ 325°F/Gas Mark 3 and place a baking sheet in the oven.

2 To make the filling, place the eggs, lemon rind and sugar in a bowl and beat together for 1 minute. Gently stir in the cream, then the lemon juice, and finally the coconut.

3 Spoon the filling into the pastry shell and place the tart tin on the preheated baking sheet. Bake in the preheated oven for 40 minutes, or until set and golden. Leave to cool for about 1 hour to firm up. Serve at room temperature.

pecan pie

serves 8   **prep: 25 mins**   **cook: 50 mins– 1 hr 5 mins**

Pecan pie is an American variation on the traditional treacle tart, and makes a rich and satisfying dessert.

INGREDIENTS

butter, for greasing

plain flour, for dusting

1 quantity Sweet Shortcrust Pastry

(see page 13)

FILLING

3 eggs

225 g/8 oz dark muscovado sugar

1 tsp vanilla essence

pinch of salt

85 g/3 oz butter, melted

3 tbsp golden syrup

3 tbsp black treacle

225 g/8 oz pecan nuts,

roughly chopped

pecan nut halves, to decorate

cream or vanilla ice cream, to serve

NUTRITIONAL INFORMATION

Calories 730

Protein 9g

Carbohydrates 74g

Sugars 53g

Fat 46g

Saturates 17g

variation

For a party-style pecan pie, pipe whipped cream over the surface in a decorative pattern before serving.

cook's tip

If the pastry is becoming too brown while the pie is cooking, cover the pie with foil to prevent it browning any further.

1 Preheat the oven to 200°C/400°F/Gas Mark 6, then grease a 23–25-cm/9–10-inch tart tin. On a lightly floured work surface, roll out the pastry and use it to line the prepared tin, then bake blind (see page 13). Reduce the oven temperature to 180°C/350°F/Gas Mark 4 and place a baking sheet in the oven.

2 To make the filling, place the eggs in a bowl and beat lightly. Beat in the sugar, vanilla essence and salt. Stir in the melted butter, syrup, treacle and chopped nuts. Pour into the pastry case and decorate with nut halves.

3 Place the tart tin on the preheated baking sheet and bake in the preheated oven for 35–40 minutes, or until the filling is set. Serve warm or at room temperature with cream or vanilla ice cream.

plum & almond tart

cook: 50 mins–1 hr 5 mins   **prep: 30 mins**   serves 8

NUTRITIONAL INFORMATION

Calories 530

Protein 8g

Carbohydrate 60g

Sugars 39g

Fat 29g

Saturates 14g

variation

As an alternative to plums, try substituting apricots, cherries or halved and sliced pears.

The flavours of plums and almonds make a particularly good combination in this delicious, warm tart.

INGREDIENTS

butter, for greasing

plain flour, for dusting

1 quantity Sweet Shortcrust Pastry (see page 13)

FILLING

1 egg

1 egg yolk

140 g/5 oz golden caster sugar

55 g/2 oz butter, melted

100 g/3½ oz ground almonds

1 tbsp brandy

900 g/2 lb plums, halved and stoned

whipped cream, to serve (optional)

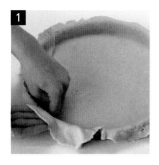

cook's tip

The plum halves need to fit together tightly because they shrink during the baking process, so make sure that there are no large gaps.

1 Preheat the oven to 200°C/400°F/Gas Mark 6, then grease a 23-cm/9-inch tart tin. On a lightly floured work surface, roll out the pastry and use it to line the tart tin, then bake blind (see page 13). Place a baking sheet in the oven.

2 To make the filling, place the egg, egg yolk, 100 g/3½ oz of the caster sugar, melted butter, ground almonds and brandy in a bowl and mix together to form a paste. Spread the paste in the pastry case.

3 Arrange the plum halves, cut-side up, on top of the almond paste, fitting them together tightly. Sprinkle with the remaining caster sugar. Place the tart tin on the preheated baking sheet and bake in the preheated oven for 35–40 minutes, or until the filling is set and the pastry is brown. Serve warm with whipped cream, if you like.

tarte au citron

serves 6   **prep: 20 mins, plus 15 mins cooling**   **cook: 40–55 mins**

This smooth, creamy tart with the tangy fresh flavour of lemons makes the perfect end to a dinner party.

INGREDIENTS

butter, for greasing

plain flour, for dusting

1 quantity Pâté Sucrée (see page 13)

FILLING

1 large egg

4 large egg yolks

140 g/5 oz golden caster sugar

finely grated rind and juice
of 4 lemons (the juice should
measure 150 ml/5 fl oz)

150 ml/5 fl oz double cream

icing sugar, for dusting

NUTRITIONAL INFORMATION

Calories 580

Protein 8g

Carbohydrate 65g

Sugars 37g

Fat 34g

Saturates 20g

variation

Reserve some of the lemon zest and sprinkle it over the tart after cooking for extra decoration.

cook's tip

The surface of the tart should not colour. If it threatens to do so while baking, cover the top loosely with a piece of foil.

1 Preheat the oven to 200°C/400°F/Gas Mark 6, then grease a 23-cm/9-inch tart tin. On a lightly floured work surface, roll out the pastry and use it to line the tart tin, then bake blind (see page 13). Reduce the oven temperature to 160°C/325°F/Gas Mark 3 and place a baking sheet in the oven.

2 To make the filling, place the egg, egg yolks and sugar in a bowl and whisk until smooth. Gently stir in the lemon rind, lemon juice and cream. Pour most of the filling into the pastry case, then place the tart tin on the preheated baking sheet in the oven and spoon in the rest of the filling.

3 Bake in the oven for 25–30 minutes, or until there is no sign of liquid movement in the filling. Leave to cool in the tin for 15 minutes and serve warm or chilled. Before serving, sift over the icing sugar to dust.

pear & cardamom tarte tatin

serves 4　　　　　**prep: 20 mins** ⏲　　　　　**cook: 30–35 mins** ♨

This is a variation on a classic French apple tart, said to have been invented by the Tatin sisters. One of them dropped an apple tart when putting it in the oven and had to cook it upside-down!

INGREDIENTS

55 g/2 oz butter, softened

55 g/2 oz golden caster sugar

seeds from 10 cardamom pods

plain flour, for dusting

225 g/8 oz ready-made puff pastry, thawed if frozen

3 ripe pears

whipped cream, to serve

NUTRITIONAL INFORMATION	
Calories	.414
Protein	.4g
Carbohydrate	.47g
Sugars	.26g
Fat	.25g
Saturates	.7g

1 Preheat the oven to 220°C/425°F/Gas Mark 7. Spread the butter over the base of an 18-cm/7-inch ovenproof omelette pan or heavy-based cake tin. Spread the sugar evenly over the butter and scatter the cardamom seeds over the sugar. On a floured work surface, roll out the pastry into a circle slightly larger than the pan. Prick the pastry lightly, place it on a plate and chill while preparing the pears.

2 Peel the pears, cut in half lengthways and cut out the cores. Arrange the pears, rounded sides down, on the butter and sugar. Set the pan over a medium heat until the sugar melts and begins to bubble with the butter and juice from the pears. If any areas are browning more than others, move the pan, but do not stir. As soon as the sugar has caramelized, remove the pan carefully from the heat.

3 Place the pastry on top, tucking the edges down the sides of the pan. Transfer to the oven and bake for 25 minutes, or until the pastry is well risen and golden. Leave the tart in the pan for 2–3 minutes, or until the juices have stopped bubbling.

4 Invert the pan over a plate and shake to release the tart. It may be necessary to slide a palette knife underneath the pears to loosen them. Serve the tart warm, with whipped cream.

treacle & orange tart

cook: 30 mins **prep: 20 mins** **serves 6**

In spite of its name, this tart contains syrup, not treacle, but the breadcrumbs give it a delicious texture, and will make it a firm family favourite.

NUTRITIONAL INFORMATION	
Calories	.275
Protein	.3g
Carbohydrate	.50g
Sugars	.27g
Fat	.8g
Saturates	.4g

INGREDIENTS

butter, for greasing

plain flour, for dusting

1 quantity Shortcrust Pastry
(see page 13)

FILLING

about 125 ml/4 fl oz golden syrup

finely grated rind of 1 orange

1 tbsp orange juice

about 6 tbsp fresh white breadcrumbs

cook's tip

When the tart is removed from the oven, the filling should still be on the soft side if the tart is to be eaten cold, because it hardens as it cools.

1 Grease a 20-cm/8-inch tart tin. On a lightly floured work surface, roll out the pastry and use it to line the tart tin. Reserve the pastry trimmings. Preheat the oven to 190°C/375°F/Gas Mark 5. To make the filling, place the syrup, orange rind and juice in a saucepan over a low heat and stir until the mixture is runny.

2 Remove the saucepan from the heat and stir in the breadcrumbs. Leave for 10 minutes, or until the breadcrumbs have absorbed the syrup. If the mixture looks stodgy, add a little more syrup; if it looks thin, add some more breadcrumbs. It should have the consistency of thick honey. Spread the mixture in the pastry case.

3 Roll out the pastry trimmings and cut into narrow strips. Use to make a lattice pattern across the top of the tart. Bake in the preheated oven for 30 minutes, or until the filling is almost set and the edge of the pastry is brown. Serve warm or cold.

makes 20 pieces

prep: 30 mins, plus 30 mins cooling

cook: 40–50 mins

Baklava is a traditional Greek pastry. Sticky and sweet and packed with nuts, it makes a delicious dessert or accompaniment to coffee.

INGREDIENTS

115 g/4 oz blanched almonds

115 g/4 oz walnuts

55 g/2 oz shelled pistachio nuts

55 g/2 oz light muscovado sugar

1 tsp ground cinnamon

½ tsp freshly grated nutmeg

55 g/2 oz butter, melted, plus extra for greasing

12 sheets ready-made filo pastry, about 30 x 18 cm/12 x 7 inches

SYRUP

225 g/8 oz granulated sugar

150 ml/5 fl oz water

1 tbsp lemon juice

1 tbsp orange flower water

NUTRITIONAL INFORMATION

Calories 190

Protein 3g

Carbohydrate 20g

Sugars 15g

Fat 11g

Saturates 2g

---

variation

You can vary the combination of nuts used for the pastry filling. Try using Brazil nuts or pecan nuts instead.

cook's tip

When chopping the nuts in the food processor, take care not to chop them into a powder – the baklava needs to have a crunchy texture.

1 To make the syrup, place the sugar, water and lemon juice in a saucepan over a low heat and stir until the sugar has completely dissolved, then boil gently for 5 minutes, until the mixture takes on a syrupy consistency. Add the orange flower water and boil for a further 2 minutes. Leave the syrup to cool completely.

2 Place one-third of all the nuts in a food processor and process until finely chopped. Roughly chop the remainder. Place all the chopped nuts in a bowl with the sugar, cinnamon and nutmeg and mix together.

3 Grease a baking tin that is roughly the same size as, or slightly smaller than, the sheets of pastry. Preheat the oven to 180°C/350°F/Gas Mark 4. Brush 1 sheet of pastry with butter and place on the bottom of the baking tin. Repeat with 3 more sheets. Spread one-third of the nut mixture over the pastry. Top with 2 more layers of buttered pastry, then another third of the nut mixture. Top with 2 more buttered filo sheets, then the remaining nuts. Top with 4 sheets of buttered filo.

4 Cut the top layer of pastry into diamonds and bake for 30–40 minutes, or until crisp and golden. Remove from the oven, pour the syrup over the top and cool. When cold, trim the edges and cut into diamond shapes.

lime & coconut meringue pie

serves 6   **prep: 30 mins** ⏲   **cook: 40–50 mins** ⏲

Rich coconut milk adds a Caribbean flavour to this variation on a traditional classic – ever-popular lemon meringue pie.

INGREDIENTS

butter, for greasing

plain flour, for dusting

1 quantity Shortcrust Pastry

(see page 13)

FILLING

4 tbsp cornflour

400 ml/14 fl oz canned coconut milk

grated rind and juice of 2 limes

2 large eggs, separated

175 g/6 oz caster sugar

zest of 1 lime, to decorate

NUTRITIONAL INFORMATION

Calories 403

Protein 6g

Carbohydrate 66g

Sugars 35g

Fat 15g

Saturates 7g

variation

Add a teaspoon of coconut liqueur to the filling with the sugar in Step 2, if you like.

cook's tip

Be careful not to overcook the meringue, otherwise it will become hard and dry rather than soft and delicious.

1 Preheat the oven to 200°C/400°F/Gas Mark 6, then grease a 23-cm/ 9-inch tart tin. On a lightly floured work surface, roll out the pastry and use it to line the tart tin, then bake blind (see page 13). Reduce the oven temperature to 160°C/ 325°F/Gas Mark 3 and place a baking sheet in the oven.

2 To make the filling, place the cornflour in a saucepan with a little of the coconut milk and stir to make a paste. Stir in the rest of the coconut milk. Bring to the boil slowly, stirring constantly. Cook over a medium–high heat, stirring, for 3 minutes, or until thickened. Remove from the heat and add the lime rind and

juice, the egg yolks and 50 g/ 1¾ oz of the caster sugar. Pour into the flan case.

3 Place the egg whites in a spotlessly clean, greasefree bowl and whisk until very stiff, then gradually whisk in the remaining caster sugar. Spread the meringue over the filling and swirl with

a palette knife. Bake in the preheated oven for 20 minutes, or until lightly browned. Decorate with lime zest and serve hot or cold.

raspberry eclairs

makes 20   **prep: 30 mins**   **cook: 40 mins**

These choux buns are perfect for serving as a dessert or in high summer at an afternoon tea.

INGREDIENTS

CHOUX PASTRY
55 g/2 oz butter

150 ml/5 fl oz water

70 g/2½ oz plain flour, sifted

2 eggs, beaten

FILLING
325 ml/11 fl oz double cream

1 tbsp icing sugar

175 g/6 oz fresh raspberries

ICING
115 g/4 oz icing sugar

2 tsp lemon juice

pink food colouring (optional)

NUTRITIONAL INFORMATION

Calories 141

Protein 2g

Carbohydrate 10g

Sugars 8g

Fat 11g

Saturates 6g

---

variation

You could use other fresh summer fruits, such as halved strawberries, for these eclairs.

cook's tip

The raw piped choux mixture can be made a few days ahead and frozen, then baked directly from the freezer for 5 minutes longer than usual.

1 Preheat the oven to 200°C/400°F/Gas Mark 6. To make the choux pastry, place the butter and water in a large, heavy-based saucepan and bring to the boil. Add the flour, all at once, and beat thoroughly until the mixture leaves the sides of the saucepan. Leave to cool slightly, then vigorously beat in the eggs, 1 at a time.

2 Spoon the mixture into a piping bag fitted with a 1-cm/½-inch nozzle and pipe 8 x 7.5-cm/3-inch lengths on to several dampened baking sheets. Bake in the preheated oven for 30 minutes, or until crisp and golden. Remove from the oven and make a small hole in each bun with the tip of a knife to let out the steam, then return to the oven for a

further 5 minutes, to dry out the insides. Transfer to a wire rack to cool.

3 To make the filling, place the cream and icing sugar in a bowl and whisk until thick. Split the buns and fill with the cream and raspberries. To make the icing, sift the icing sugar into a bowl and stir in the lemon

juice and enough water to make a smooth paste. Add pink food colouring, if desired. Drizzle the icing generously over the eclairs, and leave to set before serving.

summer fruit tartlets

makes 12 **prep: 25 mins, plus** ⏲ **30 mins chilling** **cook: 12–18 mins** ⏲

Small almond pastry cases filled with bright summer fruits taste as good as they look, with their delicate combination of flavours.

INGREDIENTS

PASTRY	FILLING
200 g/7 oz plain flour, plus extra for dusting	225 g/8 oz cream cheese
85 g/3 oz icing sugar	icing sugar, to taste, plus extra for dusting
55 g/2 oz ground almonds	350 g/12 oz fresh summer fruits, such as red- and whitecurrants, blueberries, raspberries and small strawberries
115 g/4 oz butter	
1 egg yolk	
1 tbsp milk	

NUTRITIONAL INFORMATION

Calories 280

Protein 4g

Carbohydrate 23g

Sugars 10g

Fat 20g

Saturates 11g

variation

The fruit in the tarts could be brushed with warmed redcurrant jelly to make an attractive glaze.

cook's tip

If you wash the summer fruits just before using them, be sure to drain them well on kitchen paper, otherwise the liquid will make the tartlet cases soggy.

1 To make the pastry, sift the flour and icing sugar into a bowl. Stir in the ground almonds. Add the butter and rub in until the mixture resembles breadcrumbs. Add the egg yolk and milk and work in with a palette knife, then mix with your fingers until the dough binds together. Wrap the dough in clingfilm and leave to chill in the refrigerator for 30 minutes.

2 Preheat the oven to 200°C/400°F/Gas Mark 6. On a floured work surface, roll out the pastry and use it to line 12 deep tartlet or individual brioche tins. Prick the bases. Press a piece of foil into each tartlet, covering the edges, and bake in the preheated oven for 10–15 minutes, or until light golden brown. Remove the foil and bake for a further 2–3 minutes. Transfer to a wire rack to cool.

3 To make the filling, place the cream cheese and icing sugar in a bowl and mix together. Place a spoonful of filling in each pastry case and arrange the fruit on top. Dust with sifted icing sugar and serve immediately.

pear & pecan strudel

serves 4   **prep: 15 mins**   **cook: 30–35 mins**

Crisp filo pastry is wrapped around a nutty pear filling in this easy-to-make strudel for a traditional, but unusual, dessert.

INGREDIENTS

2 ripe pears

55 g/2 oz butter, plus extra, melted, for brushing

55 g/2 oz fresh white breadcrumbs

85 g/3 oz pecan nuts, chopped

25 g/1 oz light muscovado sugar

finely grated rind of 1 orange

100 g/3½ oz ready-made filo pastry

70 g/2½ oz orange blossom honey

2 tbsp orange juice

icing sugar, for dusting

Greek yogurt, to serve

NUTRITIONAL INFORMATION

Calories	.466
Protein	.6g
Carbohydrate	.52g
Sugars	.30g
Fat	.28g
Saturates	.9g

cook's tip

When working with filo pastry, it is important to keep it covered until you are ready to use it, otherwise it will dry out very quickly.

1 Preheat the oven to 200°C/400°F/Gas Mark 6. Peel, core and chop the pears. Place 15 g/½ oz of the butter in a frying pan over a low heat, add the breadcrumbs and gently fry until golden. Transfer the breadcrumbs to a bowl and add the chopped pears with the nuts, sugar and orange rind. Place the remaining butter in a small saucepan and heat until melted.

2 Keep 1 sheet of filo pastry back, keeping it well wrapped, and layer the remaining filo sheets on a clean work surface, brushing each one with a little melted butter. Spoon the nut filling on to the filo sheets, leaving a 2.5-cm/1-inch margin around the edges. Drizzle with the honey and orange juice.

3 Fold the short ends over the filling, then roll up, beginning at a long side. Lift on to a baking sheet, seam-side up. Brush with any remaining melted butter and crumple the remaining sheet of filo pastry around the strudel.

Bake in the preheated oven for 25 minutes, or until golden and crisp. Dust with sifted icing sugar and serve warm with Greek yogurt.

sicilian ricotta tart

⏱ **cook: 1 hr 25 mins– 1 hr 40 mins**   ⏱ **prep: 15 mins**   **serves 6**

Pine kernels and mixed peel are included in the filling of this Italian speciality.

NUTRITIONAL INFORMATION

Calories	.207
Protein	.8g
Carbohydrate	.16g
Sugars	.16g
Fat	.13g
Saturates	.4g

INGREDIENTS

butter, for greasing

plain flour, for dusting

1 quantity Pâté Sucrée (see page 13)

FILLING

250 g/9 oz ricotta cheese

2 eggs, beaten

55 g/2 oz golden caster sugar

55 g/2 oz pine kernels

55 g/2 oz chopped mixed peel

finely grated rind of 1 lemon

½ tsp vanilla essence

icing sugar, for dusting

cook's tip

If possible, it is best to buy packets of whole pieces of mixed peel, if your local supermarket stocks them, and chop them up yourself.

1 Preheat the oven to 200°C/400°F/Gas Mark 6, then grease a 20-cm/8-inch tart tin. On a lightly floured work surface, roll out the pastry and use it to line the tin, then bake blind (see page 13). Reduce the oven temperature to 180°C/350°F/Gas Mark 4 and place a baking sheet in the oven.

2 To make the filling, press the ricotta cheese through a sieve into a bowl. Add the eggs, sugar, pine kernels, mixed peel, lemon rind and vanilla essence. Mix well, then pour into the pastry case.

3 Place the tart on the preheated baking sheet and bake in the preheated oven for 45 minutes, or until lightly set. Leave to cool, then dust with sifted icing sugar and serve.

chocolate, chestnut & ginger tart

serves 8 **prep: 30 mins, plus 1–2 hrs chilling** **cook: 45 mins**

The biscuit-crumb tart case used in this recipe is ideal if you do not want to go to the trouble of making pastry.

INGREDIENTS

BISCUIT CASE
85 g/3 oz butter

250 g/9 oz ginger snap biscuits, crushed

FILLING
175 g/6 oz unsweetened chestnut purée

55 g/2 oz golden caster sugar

175 g/6 oz ricotta cheese

2 eggs

100 g/3½ oz plain chocolate, melted

55 g/2 oz preserved ginger, cut into tiny slivers

25 g/1 oz ground almonds

TO DECORATE
150 ml/5 fl oz whipping cream

chocolate curls

variation

Substitute the chocolate decoration with slivers of preserved ginger or a sprinkling of ground ginger mixed with sweet drinking chocolate powder.

cook's tip

You can use other types of biscuits to make a biscuit base for a flan, such as digestives. To work well, the biscuits need to be fairly rich and buttery.

1 Preheat the oven to 180°C/350°F/Gas Mark 4. Place the butter in a saucepan over a low heat until just melted. Stir in the crushed biscuits. Press the crumbs on to the base and up the sides of a 23-cm/9-inch loose-bottomed flan tin. Bake in the preheated oven for 10 minutes, then leave to cool. Leave the oven switched on.

2 To make the filling, place the chestnut purée and sugar in a bowl and beat until smooth. Place the ricotta cheese and eggs in a separate bowl and beat until smooth. Carefully stir the melted chocolate into the ricotta mixture. Add the chestnut purée mixture and mix thoroughly. Stir in the ginger and ground almonds.

3 Pour the filling into the biscuit case and bake in the preheated oven for 35 minutes, or until lightly set. Leave to cool, then chill in the refrigerator for 1–2 hours.

4 Before serving, place the cream in a bowl and whip until thick. Spread over the top of the tart and sprinkle with chocolate curls.

maple pecan tarts

makes 14   **prep: 20 mins, plus** ⏲ **10–30 mins cooling**   **cook: 20–25 mins** ⏲

Rich maple syrup and pecan nuts give a wonderful flavour to the toffee filling in these moreish little tarts.

INGREDIENTS

PASTRY

140 g/5 oz plain flour, plus extra for dusting

85 g/3 oz butter

55 g/2 oz golden caster sugar

2 egg yolks

FILLING

2 tbsp maple syrup

150 ml/5 fl oz double cream

115 g/4 oz golden caster sugar

pinch of cream of tartar

75 ml/2½ fl oz water

115 g/4 oz pecan nuts

14 pecan nut halves, to decorate

NUTRITIONAL INFORMATION

Calories	.268
Protein	.3g
Carbohydrate	.23g
Sugars	.15g
Fat	.19g
Saturates	.7g

variation

Pipe whipped cream around the edges of the cooled tarts for a more decorative presentation.

cook's tip

It is important to use genuine maple syrup rather than the readily-available maple-flavoured syrup, to make sure that the tarts are rich and flavoursome.

1 Sift the flour into a large bowl, then cut the butter into pieces and rub it into the flour using your fingertips until the mixture resembles breadcrumbs. Stir in the sugar, then stir in the egg yolks to make a smooth dough. Wrap in clingfilm and leave to chill in the refrigerator for 30 minutes.

2 Preheat the oven to 200°C/400°F/Gas Mark 6. On a floured work surface, roll out the pastry thinly, cut out circles and use to line 12 tartlet tins. Prick the bases and press a piece of foil into each pastry case. Bake in the oven for 10–15 minutes, or until light golden. Remove the foil and bake for 2–3 minutes. Cool on a wire rack.

3 To make the filling, place half the maple syrup and half the cream in a bowl and mix together. Place the sugar, cream of tartar and water in a saucepan over a low heat and stir until the sugar dissolves. Bring to the boil and continue boiling until light golden. Remove from the heat and stir in the maple syrup and cream mixture.

4 Return to the heat and cook to the 'soft ball' stage (116°C/240°F), when a little of the mixture forms a soft ball when dropped into cold water. Stir in the remaining cream and leave until warm. Brush the remaining syrup over the edges of the tarts. Place the pecan nuts in the cases, spoon in the toffee and top with a nut half. Leave to cool.

crab & ginger triangles

makes 12   **prep: 15–20 mins** ⏲   **cook: 20–25 mins** ♨

These crisp little crab parcels could be served as an unusual starter at a dinner party, or as a snack at a buffet or with drinks.

INGREDIENTS

85 g/3 oz butter, melted, plus
extra for greasing
200 g/7 oz fresh or canned
crabmeat, drained
6 spring onions, finely chopped, plus
extra to garnish
2.5-cm/1-inch piece of fresh root
ginger, peeled and grated
2 tsp soy sauce
pepper
12 sheets ready-made filo pastry

NUTRITIONAL INFORMATION

Calories	.105
Protein	.4g
Carbohydrate	.8g
Sugars	.1g
Fat	.6g
Saturates	.4g

cook's tip

It is a good idea to use fresh crabmeat for this recipe, if it is available, instead of less flavoursome canned crabmeat.

1 Preheat the oven to 180°C/350°F/Gas Mark 4, then grease a baking sheet. Place the crabmeat, spring onions, ginger and soy sauce in a bowl, add pepper to taste, mix together and reserve. Working with 1 sheet of filo pastry at a time and keeping the rest covered with a cloth, brush a pastry sheet with melted butter, fold in half lengthways and brush again with butter.

2 Place a spoonful of the crab mixture in one corner of the pastry strip. Fold the pastry and filling over at right angles to make a triangle enclosing the filling. Continue folding in this way all the way down the strip to make a triangular parcel.

3 Place the parcel on the prepared baking sheet. Repeat with the remaining pastry and crab mixture. Brush each parcel with melted butter. Bake in the preheated oven for 20–25 minutes, or until crisp and golden brown. Garnish with extra chopped spring onions and serve warm.

filo tartlets with avocado salsa

⏱ **cook: 6–8 mins**　　　　⏱ **prep: 20 mins**　　　　**makes 20**

Filo pastry makes crisp little containers for a spicy avocado salsa. If you are making these for a party, fill them just before serving.

NUTRITIONAL INFORMATION	
Calories 49	
Protein 1g	
Carbohydrate 3g	
Sugars 1g	
Fat 4g	
Saturates 2g	

INGREDIENTS

TARTLET CASES

70 g/2½ oz ready-made filo pastry

3 tbsp melted butter, plus

extra for greasing

AVOCADO SALSA

1 large avocado

1 small red onion, finely chopped

1 fresh chilli, deseeded and

finely chopped

2 tomatoes, peeled, deseeded and

finely chopped

juice of 1 lime

2 tbsp chopped fresh coriander

salt and pepper

cook's tip

The pastry cases can be made up to a week in advance and stored in an airtight container. Make the salsa just before serving. Once the cases are filled, serve them straight away, otherwise they will go soft.

1 Preheat the oven to 180°C/350°F/Gas Mark 4. To make the tartlet cases, working with 1 sheet of filo pastry at a time and keeping the rest covered with a cloth, brush the pastry sheet with melted butter. With a sharp knife, cut the sheet into 5-cm/2-inch squares.

2 Grease 20 cups in mini muffin trays and line each one with 3 buttered filo pastry squares, setting each one at an angle to the others. Repeat until all the pastry is used up. Bake in the preheated oven for 6–8 minutes, or until crisp and golden. Carefully transfer to a wire rack to cool.

3 To make the salsa, peel the avocado and remove the stone. Cut the flesh into small dice and place in a bowl with the onion, chilli, tomatoes, lime juice and coriander, and add salt and pepper to taste. Divide the salsa between the pastry cases and serve immediately.

mini choux puffs with prawn cocktail

makes 22   **prep: 30 mins** ⟳   **cook: 35 mins** ⟳

Prawn cocktail is making a comeback, but here it is given a new look, served in mini choux buns as a cocktail snack.

INGREDIENTS

CHOUX PASTRY
55 g/2 oz butter, plus extra for greasing
150 ml/5 fl oz water
70 g/2½ oz plain flour, sifted
2 eggs, beaten

FILLING
2 tbsp mayonnaise
1 tsp tomato purée
140 g/5 oz small prawns, cooked and peeled
1 tsp Worcestershire sauce
salt
Tabasco sauce
1 Little Gem lettuce, shredded
cayenne pepper, to garnish

NUTRITIONAL INFORMATION

Calories 65

Protein 3g

Carbohydrate 3g

Sugars 0g

Fat 5g

Saturates 2g

---

variation

If you prefer, garnish with thin slivers of red pepper instead of the cayenne pepper.

cook's tip

The choux puffs can be filled up to 3 hours in advance, then left in the refrigerator until you are ready to serve them. Bring them to room temperature before serving.

1 Preheat the oven to 180°C/350°F/Gas Mark 4, then grease a baking sheet. To make the choux pastry, place the butter and water in a large, heavy-based saucepan and bring to the boil. Add the flour, all at once, and beat thoroughly until the mixture leaves the sides of the saucepan. Leave to cool slightly, then vigorously beat in the eggs, 1 at a time. Place 22 walnut-sized spoonfuls of the mixture on to the baking sheet, spaced 2 cm/¾ inch apart. Bake in the preheated oven for 35 minutes, or until light, crisp and golden. Transfer to a wire rack to cool, then cut a 5-mm/¼-inch slice from the top of each puff.

2 To make the filling, place the mayonnaise, tomato purée, prawns and Worcestershire sauce in a bowl. Add salt and Tabasco sauce to taste, and mix together until combined.

3 Place a few lettuce shreds in the bottom of each puff, making sure some protrude at the top. Spoon the prawn mixture on top and dust with a little cayenne pepper before serving.

greek feta & olive tartlets

makes 12 **prep: 30 mins** **cook: 30 mins**

Tangy feta cheese and fruity olives make a tasty filling for these baby quiches, which are ideal for party buffets.

INGREDIENTS

butter, for greasing

plain flour, for dusting

1 quantity Shortcrust Pastry

(see page 13)

1 egg

3 egg yolks

300 ml/10 fl oz whipping cream

salt and pepper

115 g/4 oz feta cheese

6 stoned black olives, halved

12 small fresh rosemary sprigs

NUTRITIONAL INFORMATION	
Calories 208	
Protein 4g	
Carbohydrate 8g	
Sugars 1g	
Fat 18g	
Saturates 9g	

cook's tip

Feta cheese is quite salty so there is no need to add much extra salt when you season the egg mixture in Step 2.

1 Preheat the oven to 200°C/400°F/Gas Mark 6. Grease 12 individual 6-cm/2½-inch tart tins, or the cups in a 12-hole bun tray. On a floured work surface, roll out the pastry to 3 mm/⅛ inch thick. Use to line the prepared tins and prick the bases with a fork. Press a square of foil into each pastry case and bake in the preheated oven for

12 minutes. Remove the foil and bake for a further 3 minutes.

2 Place the egg, egg yolks and cream in a bowl, add salt and pepper to taste and beat together.

3 Crumble the feta cheese into the pastry cases and spoon over the egg

mixture. Place half an olive and a rosemary sprig on top of each tartlet, then bake in the oven for 15 minutes, or until the filling is just set. Serve warm or cold.

instant pesto & goat's cheese tartlets

cook: 10 mins   **prep: 15 mins**   **makes 20**

The puff pastry in these tartlets rises up round the flavoursome filling to make an instant pastry case!

NUTRITIONAL INFORMATION	
Calories 66	
Protein 2g	
Carbohydrate 4g	
Sugars 1g	
Fat 5g	
Saturates 1g	

INGREDIENTS

200 g/7 oz ready-made puff pastry

plain flour, for dusting

3 tbsp pesto

20 cherry tomatoes, each cut into 3 slices

115 g/4 oz goat's cheese

salt and pepper

fresh basil sprigs, to garnish

cook's tip

These tartlets are even quicker to make if you use the ready-rolled variety of ready-made puff pastry, which is available in most large supermarkets.

1 Preheat the oven to 200°C/400°F/Gas Mark 6, then lightly flour a baking sheet. Roll out the pastry on a floured work surface to 3 mm/⅛ inch thick. Cut out 20 rounds with a 5-cm/2-inch plain cutter and arrange the pastry rounds on the floured baking sheet.

2 Spread a little pesto on each round, leaving a margin around the edges, then arrange 3 tomato slices on top of each one.

3 Crumble the goat's cheese over and season to taste with salt and pepper.

Bake in the preheated oven for 10 minutes, or until the pastry is puffed up, crisp and golden. Garnish with basil sprigs and serve warm.

small cakes

If the thought of small cakes makes you think of tiered cake racks filled with over-sweet 'fancies' covered in pink icing or rolled in desiccated coconut, think again. This collection of irresistible cake recipes will have you rushing into the kitchen to start baking immediately.

Small cakes are very quick and easy to make, as they do not take long to cook and they are made from simple ingredients. If you have not tasted fairy cakes since childhood birthday parties, it is time to rediscover their delights, for fairy cakes have grown up and are now piled up and served at the most sophisticated gatherings. Enjoy the unusual fragrance of Lavender Fairy Cakes (see page 102) or tangy Lemon Butterfly Cakes (see page 104). Many of the easiest cakes in this section, such as Cappuccino Squares (see page 106), Walnut & Cinnamon Blondies (see page 108) or Mincemeat Crumble Bars (see page 110), are baked as tray-bakes in one large tin, then cut into squares to serve. These are also ideal for cake stalls at fêtes and fund-raising events, but you might need to hide them from the family if you don't want them to disappear before you get them packed up. Meringues are always great favourites, and there are recipes here for Brown Sugar Meringues (see page 113) with a lovely caramel flavour and delicate Strawberry Rose Meringues (see page 114). Traditional tea-time fare such as Buttermilk Scones (see page 122), griddle-cooked Welsh Cakes (see page 124) and Scotch pancakes with orange butter (see page 126) are also included, alongside recipes for mouthwatering American-style muffins. savoury Cheese Muffins (see page 129) or Bacon & Polenta Muffins (see page 128) are ideal for serving at breakfast or to accompany soups.

lavender fairy cakes

makes 12   **prep: 15 mins, plus ⏲ 20 mins cooling**   **cook: 12–15 mins ⏱**

Lavender might seem like an unusual ingredient, but it gives a special fragrance and flavour to these little cakes.

INGREDIENTS

115 g/4 oz golden caster sugar

115 g/4 oz butter, softened

2 eggs, beaten

1 tbsp milk

1 tsp finely chopped lavender flowers

½ tsp vanilla essence

175 g/6 oz self-raising flour, sifted

140 g/5 oz icing sugar

TO DECORATE

lavender flowers

silver dragées

NUTRITIONAL INFORMATION

Calories 217

Protein 3g

Carbohydrate 33g

Sugars 23g

Fat 9g

Saturates 6g

variation

Add a little purple food colouring to the icing to give it a pale lilac colour to complement the lavender.

cook's tip

Always make sure that your lavender flowers are suitable to eat and free from any chemical sprays or insecticides.

1 Preheat the oven to 200°C/400°F/Gas Mark 6. Place 12 paper cake cases in a bun tin. Place the caster sugar and butter in a bowl and cream together until pale and fluffy. Gradually beat in the eggs. Stir in the milk, lavender and vanilla essence, then carefully fold in the flour.

2 Divide the mixture between the paper cases and bake in the oven for 12–15 minutes, or until well risen and golden. The sponge should bounce back when pressed. A few minutes before the cakes are ready, sift the icing sugar into a bowl and stir in enough water to make a thick icing.

3 When the cakes are baked, transfer to a wire rack and place a blob of icing in the centre of each one, allowing it to run across the cake. Decorate with lavender flowers and silver dragées and serve as soon as the cakes are cool.

lemon butterfly cakes

makes 12　　　　**prep: 20 mins, plus 30 mins cooling**　　　　**cook: 15–20 mins**

Butterfly cakes may remind you of children's parties, but these attractive, creamy, miniature delights are for adults too!

INGREDIENTS

115 g/4 oz self-raising flour

½ tsp baking powder

115 g/4 oz butter, softened

115 g/4 oz golden caster sugar

2 eggs, beaten

finely grated rind of ½ lemon

2–4 tbsp milk

icing sugar, for dusting

FILLING

55 g/2 oz butter

115 g/4 oz icing sugar

1 tbsp lemon juice

NUTRITIONAL INFORMATION

Calories 227

Protein 2g

Carbohydrate 28g

Sugars 20g

Fat 13g

Saturates 8g

variation

To make these cakes extra special, place a few slices of strawberry on top of each one.

cook's tip

If time is limited and you want to speed things up, then the cake mixture could be mixed in a food processor, rather than by hand.

1 Preheat the oven to 190°C/375°F/Gas Mark 5. Place 12 paper cases in a bun tin. Sift the flour and baking powder into a bowl. Add the butter, sugar, eggs, lemon rind and enough milk to give a medium–soft consistency. Beat the mixture thoroughly until smooth, then divide between the paper cases and bake in the preheated oven for 15–20 minutes, or until well risen and golden. Transfer to wire racks to cool.

2 To make the filling, place the butter in a bowl. Sift in the icing sugar and add the lemon juice. Beat well until smooth and creamy. When the cakes are quite cold, use a sharp-pointed vegetable knife to cut a circle from the top of each cake, then cut each circle in half.

3 Spoon a little buttercream into the centre of each cake and press the 2 semi-circular pieces into it to resemble wings. Dust the cakes with sifted icing sugar before serving.

cappuccino squares

makes 15

prep: 10 mins, plus 30 mins cooling

cook: 35–40 mins

These cakes are made by the all-in-one method and baked in one tin, so they are very easy to put together. They are perfect for the cake stall at fêtes, or for bring-and-buy sales.

INGREDIENTS

225 g/8 oz butter, softened, plus extra for greasing

225 g/8 oz self-raising flour

1 tsp baking powder

1 tsp cocoa powder, plus extra for dusting

225 g/8 oz golden caster sugar

4 eggs, beaten

3 tbsp instant coffee granules dissolved in 2 tbsp hot water

cocoa powder, for dusting

WHITE CHOCOLATE FROSTING

115 g/4 oz white chocolate, broken into pieces

55 g/2 oz butter, softened

3 tbsp milk

175 g/6 oz icing sugar

NUTRITIONAL INFORMATION

Calories 357

Protein 4g

Carbohydrate 44g

Sugars 33g

Fat 20g

Saturates 12g

---

variation

Use chocolate coffee beans as an extra decoration, placing one chocolate bean on each square.

---

cook's tip

When melting the frosting ingredients, make sure that the base of the bowl does not touch the simmering water, otherwise the chocolate will seize and become unusable.

1 Preheat the oven to 180°C/350°F/Gas Mark 4. Grease and line the base of a shallow 28 x 18-cm/ 11 x 7-inch tin. Sift the flour, baking powder and cocoa into a bowl and add the butter, caster sugar, eggs and coffee. Beat well, by hand or with an electric whisk, until smooth, then spoon into the prepared tin and smooth the top.

2 Bake in the oven for 35–40 minutes, or until risen and firm. Leave to cool in the tin for 10 minutes, then turn out on to a wire rack and peel off the lining paper. Leave to cool completely. To make the frosting, place the chocolate, butter and milk in a bowl set over a saucepan of simmering water and stir until the chocolate has melted.

3 Remove the bowl from the saucepan and sift in the icing sugar. Beat until smooth, then spread over the cake. Dust the top of the cake with sifted cocoa powder, then cut into squares.

walnut & cinnamon blondies

makes 9 | **prep: 10 mins, plus 30 mins cooling** | **cook: 25–30 mins**

Blondies are brownies without the chocolate! They taste just as delicious served with a hot cup of coffee.

INGREDIENTS

115 g/4 oz butter, plus extra for greasing

225 g/8 oz light muscovado sugar

1 egg

1 egg yolk

140 g/5 oz self-raising flour

1 tsp ground cinnamon

85 g/3 oz walnuts, roughly chopped

NUTRITIONAL INFORMATION

Calories 325

Protein 4g

Carbohydrate 38g

Sugars 27g

Fat 18g

Saturates 8g

cook's tip

Do not chop the walnuts too finely, as the blondies should have a good texture and a slight crunch to them.

1 Preheat the oven to 180°C/350°F/Gas Mark 4. Grease and line the base of an 18-cm/7-inch square cake tin. Place the butter and sugar in a saucepan over a low heat and stir until the sugar has dissolved. Cook, stirring, for a further 1 minute. The mixture will bubble slightly, but do not let it boil. Leave to cool for 10 minutes.

2 Stir the egg and egg yolk into the mixture. Sift in the flour and cinnamon, add the nuts and stir until just blended. Pour the cake mixture into the prepared tin, then bake in the preheated oven for 20–25 minutes, or until springy in the centre and a skewer inserted into the centre of the cake comes out clean.

3 Leave to cool in the tin for a few minutes, then run a knife around the edge of the cake to loosen it. Turn the cake out on to a wire rack and peel off the paper. Leave to cool completely. When cold, cut into squares.

mocha brownies

cook: 30–35 mins　　　　**prep: 10 mins, plus 30 mins cooling**　　　　**makes 16**

A hint of coffee gives these brownies a sophisticated flavour. They make an ideal mid-afternoon treat.

NUTRITIONAL INFORMATION

Calories	160
Protein	2g
Carbohydrate	21g
Sugars	16g
Fat	8g
Saturates	4g

INGREDIENTS

55 g/2 oz butter, plus extra
for greasing
115 g/4 oz plain chocolate,
broken into pieces
175 g/6 oz dark muscovado sugar
2 eggs
1 tbsp instant coffee granules
dissolved in 1 tbsp hot water, cooled
85 g/3 oz plain flour
½ tsp baking powder
55 g/2 oz pecan nuts, roughly chopped

cook's tip

The brownies will sink slightly and crack as they cool – this is perfectly normal, and gives them their delicious, dense texture.

1 Preheat the oven to 180°C/350°F/Gas Mark 4. Grease and line the base of a 20-cm/8-inch square cake tin. Place the chocolate and butter in a heavy-based saucepan over a low heat until melted. Stir and leave to cool.

2 Place the sugar and eggs in a large bowl and cream together until light and fluffy. Fold in the chocolate mixture and cooled coffee and mix thoroughly. Sift in the flour and baking powder and lightly fold into the mixture. Carefully fold in the pecan nuts.

3 Pour the mixture into the prepared tin and bake in the preheated oven for 25–30 minutes, or until firm and a skewer inserted into the centre comes out clean.

4 Leave to cool in the tin for a few minutes, then run a knife around the edge of the cake to loosen it. Turn the cake out on to a wire rack and peel off the lining paper. Leave to cool completely. When cold, cut into squares.

mincemeat crumble bars

makes 12   **prep: 20 mins, plus** 🕒 **1 hr chilling/cooling**   **cook: 32–35 mins** 🕒

These crumble bars make a change from standard, traditional mince pies at Christmas, but don't just serve them over the festive season; they will be popular at any time of year!

INGREDIENTS

400 g/14 oz ready-made mincemeat
icing sugar, for dusting

BASE
140 g/5 oz butter, plus
extra for greasing
85 g/3 oz golden caster sugar
140 g/5 oz plain flour
85 g/3 oz cornflour

TOPPING
115 g/4 oz self-raising flour
85 g/3 oz butter, cut into pieces
85 g/3 oz golden caster sugar
25 g/1 oz flaked almonds

variation

Add a teaspoon of ground cinnamon or ground mixed spice to the topping mix for a little extra flavour.

cook's tip

Make sure that you bake the base thoroughly. If it is undercooked, it will not be crisp enough.

1 Grease a shallow 28 x 20-cm/11 x 8-inch cake tin. To make the base, place the butter and sugar in a bowl and cream together until light and fluffy. Sift in the flour and cornflour and, with your hands, bring the mixture together to form a ball. Push the dough into the prepared tin, pressing it out and into the corners with your fingers, then leave to chill in the refrigerator for 20 minutes. Preheat the oven to 200°C/400°F/Gas Mark 6. After chilling, bake the base in the oven for 12–15 minutes, or until puffed and golden.

2 To make the crumble topping, place the flour, butter and sugar in a bowl and rub together to form rough crumbs. Stir in the almonds.

3 Spread the mincemeat over the base and scatter the crumbs on top. Bake in the oven for a further 20 minutes, or until golden brown. Leave to cool slightly, then cut into 12 pieces and leave to cool completely. Dust with sifted icing sugar, then serve.

coconut & cherry cakes

makes 8　　　**prep: 15 mins, plus 20 mins cooling**　　　**cook: 20–25 mins**

Coconut makes these little cakes very moist, and gives them a sweet flavour that will make them a hit with children.

INGREDIENTS

115 g/4 oz butter, softened

115 g/4 oz golden caster sugar

2 tbsp milk

2 eggs, beaten

85 g/3 oz self-raising flour

½ tsp baking powder

85 g/3 oz desiccated coconut

115 g/4 oz glacé cherries, quartered

NUTRITIONAL INFORMATION

Calories 320

Protein 4g

Carbohydrate 34g

Sugars 26g

Fat 20g

Saturates 14g

variation

Currants, chopped dried apricots or dried blueberries could be used instead of cherries.

1 Preheat the oven to 180°C/350°F/Gas Mark 4. Line 1 or 2 muffin trays with 8 paper muffin cases. Place the butter and sugar in a bowl and cream together until light and fluffy, then stir in the milk.

2 Gradually beat in the eggs. Sift in the flour and baking powder and fold in with the coconut. Gently fold in most of the cherries. Spoon the mixture into the paper cases and scatter the remaining cherries on top.

3 Bake in the preheated oven for 20–25 minutes, or until well risen, golden and firm to the touch. Transfer to a wire rack to cool.

brown sugar meringues

cook: 2–3 hrs

prep: 30 mins, plus 20 mins cooling

makes 18

The muscovado sugar in these meringues creates a wonderful rich caramel flavour while they are baking.

NUTRITIONAL INFORMATION	
Calories	102
Protein	1g
Carbohydrate	11g
Sugars	11g
Fat	7g
Saturates	4g

INGREDIENTS

3 egg whites

175 g/6 oz light muscovado sugar, sifted, plus extra for sprinkling

300 ml/10 fl oz whipping cream

variation

For hazelnut meringues, sprinkle chopped toasted hazelnuts over the meringues before baking.

1 Preheat the oven to 110°C/225°F/Gas Mark ¼. Line 2 large baking sheets with non-stick baking paper. Place the egg whites in a large, spotlessly clean, greasefree bowl and whisk until stiff peaks form.

2 Very gradually whisk in the sugar, a spoonful at a time, making sure that you whisk the mixture well between each addition to ensure that the sugar has dissolved and blended with the egg whites. Place spoonfuls of the mixture on the prepared baking sheets. Sprinkle a little sugar on top of each one.

3 Bake in the preheated oven for 2–3 hours, or until dry, swapping over the baking sheets halfway through the cooking time. Leave to cool. Place the cream in a bowl and whip until thick. Sandwich the meringues together in pairs with the cream and serve.

strawberry rose meringues

makes 12   **prep: 30 mins, plus 20 mins cooling**   **cook: 1 hr**

Rosewater gives an exotic fragrance to the delicious whipped cream filling in these attractive strawberry meringues.

INGREDIENTS

2 egg whites

115 g/4 oz caster sugar

FILLING

55 g/2 oz strawberries

2 tsp icing sugar

3 tbsp rosewater

150 ml/5 fl oz double cream

TO DECORATE

12 fresh strawberries

rose petals

NUTRITIONAL INFORMATION

Calories 104

Protein 1g

Carbohydrate 12g

Sugars 12g

Fat 6g

Saturates 4g

variation

You can substitute raspberries for the strawberries, or use a mixture of the 2 fruits, if you like.

cook's tip

When sugar is whisked into egg whites to make a meringue, it should gradually dissolve into the egg whites. Make sure the bowl is very clean, otherwise the meringue will not hold its shape.

1 Preheat the oven to 110°C/225°F/Gas Mark ¼. Line 2 large baking sheets with non-stick baking paper. Place the egg whites in a large, spotlessly clean, greasefree bowl and whisk until stiff peaks form. Whisk in half the sugar, then carefully fold in the remainder.

2 Spoon the meringue into a piping bag fitted with a large star nozzle. Pipe 24 x 7.5-cm/3-inch lengths on to the baking sheets. Bake in the oven for 1 hour, or until the meringues are dry and crisp. Cool on wire racks.

3 To make the filling, place the strawberries in a blender or food processor and process to a purée. Sieve the purée into a bowl and stir in the icing sugar and rosewater. Place the cream in a separate bowl and whip until thick. Stir into the strawberry mixture and mix well together.

4 Sandwich the meringues together with the strawberry cream.

Cut 6 of the strawberries for the decoration in half and use to decorate the meringues. Scatter rose petals over the top and serve immediately with the remaining whole strawberries.

cherry & sultana rockies

makes 10   **prep: 10 mins, plus 30 mins cooling**   **cook: 10–15 mins**

*Rock cakes are always popular, and are quick and easy to make.
To be at their best, they should be eaten the day they are made.*

INGREDIENTS

85 g/3 oz butter, plus extra for greasing

250 g/9 oz self-raising flour

1 tsp ground mixed spice

85 g/3 oz golden caster sugar

55 g/2 oz glacé cherries, quartered

55 g/2 oz sultanas

1 egg

2 tbsp milk

demerara sugar, for sprinkling

NUTRITIONAL INFORMATION

Calories 224

Protein 3g

Carbohydrate 37g

Sugars 18g

Fat 8g

Saturates 5g

---

variation

Mixed dried fruit could be used as an alternative to the cherries and sultanas in these rock cakes.

---

cook's tip

Rockies are a cross between a biscuit and a cake. When you place the uncooked mixture on the baking sheet, do not worry about making neat piles – they should look rocky, as their name implies!

1 Preheat the oven to 200°C/400°F/Gas Mark 6, then grease a baking sheet. Sift the flour and mixed spice into a bowl. Add the butter and rub in until the mixture resembles breadcrumbs. Stir in the sugar, cherries and sultanas.

2 Break the egg into a bowl and whisk in the milk. Pour most of the egg mixture into the dry ingredients and mix with a fork to make a stiff, rough dough, adding the rest of the egg and milk, if necessary.

3 Using 2 forks, pile the mixture into 10 rocky heaps on the prepared baking sheet. Sprinkle with demerara sugar. Bake in the preheated oven for 10–15 minutes, or until golden brown and firm to the touch. Leave to cool on the baking sheet for 2 minutes, then transfer to a wire rack to cool completely.

apple & cinnamon muffins

makes 6   **prep: 15 mins** ⏲   **cook: 20–25 mins** ⏲

These spicy muffins are quick and easy to make with a few stock ingredients and two small apples. The crunchy sugar topping turns them into a truly fruity treat.

INGREDIENTS

85 g/3 oz plain wholemeal flour

70 g/2½ oz plain white flour

1½ tsp baking powder

pinch of salt

1 tsp ground cinnamon

40 g/1½ oz golden caster sugar

2 small eating apples, peeled, cored and finely chopped

125 ml/4 fl oz milk

1 egg, beaten

55 g/2 oz butter, melted

TOPPING

12 brown sugar cubes, roughly crushed

½ tsp ground cinnamon

NUTRITIONAL INFORMATION

Calories 250

Protein 5g

Carbohydrate 38g

Sugars 20g

Fat 10g

Saturates 6g

---

variation

If you like, you can split this mixture into 12 portions to make small muffins.

cook's tip

Work quickly once you have chopped the apple, as the flesh soon begins to brown on exposure to the air.

1 Preheat the oven to 200°C/400°F/Gas Mark 6. Line 6 holes of a muffin tray with paper muffin cases.

2 Sift the 2 flours, baking powder, salt and cinnamon into a large bowl and stir in the sugar and chopped apples. Place the milk, egg and butter in a separate bowl and mix. Add the wet ingredients to the dry ingredients and gently stir until just combined.

3 Divide the mixture between the paper cases. To make the topping, mix together the crushed sugar cubes and cinnamon and sprinkle over the muffins. Bake in the preheated oven for 20–25 minutes, or until risen and golden. Serve the muffins warm or cold.

triple chocolate muffins

makes 11　　　　**prep: 15 mins** ⏱　　　　**cook: 20 mins** ⏱

Packed with melting plain and white chocolate, these creamy muffins are a chocoholic's delight.

INGREDIENTS

250 g/9 oz plain flour

25 g/1 oz cocoa powder

2 tsp baking powder

½ tsp bicarbonate of soda

100 g/3½ oz plain chocolate chips

100 g/3½ oz white chocolate chips

2 eggs, beaten

300 ml/10 fl oz soured cream

85 g/3 oz light muscovado sugar

85 g/3 oz butter, melted

NUTRITIONAL INFORMATION	
Calories	.340
Protein	.6g
Carbohydrate	.39g
Sugars	.20g
Fat	.19g
Saturates	.11g

cook's tip

As with all muffins, these chocolate delights taste best if they are eaten fresh, on the day they are made.

1 Preheat the oven to 200°C/400°F/Gas Mark 6. Line 11 holes of 1 or 2 muffin trays with paper muffin cases. Sift the flour, cocoa powder, baking powder and bicarbonate of soda into a large bowl, add the plain and white chocolate chips and stir.

2 Place the eggs, soured cream, sugar and butter in a separate bowl and mix. Add the wet ingredients to the dry ingredients and stir gently until just combined.

3 Using 2 forks, divide the mixture between the paper cases and bake in the preheated oven for 20 minutes, or until well risen and firm to the touch. Serve warm or cold.

lemon & ricotta pancakes

 cook: 20–30 mins   prep: 10 mins   makes 15

These thick, soft pancakes can be served for breakfast or lunch, or as a delicious and unusual dessert.

NUTRITIONAL INFORMATION	
Calories	.88
Protein	.3g
Carbohydrate	.8g
Sugars	.6g
Fat	.5g
Saturates	.3g

INGREDIENTS

250 g/9 oz ricotta cheese

5 tbsp golden caster sugar

3 large eggs, separated

finely grated rind of 1 lemon

2 tbsp melted butter

55 g/2 oz plain flour

warmed cherry or blueberry conserve,
to serve

cook's tip

Do not spread the pancake mixture too thinly in the frying pan – the finished pancakes should be about 10–13 cm/ 4–5 inches across.

1 Place the ricotta cheese, sugar and egg yolks in a large bowl and mix together. Stir in the lemon rind and melted butter. Sift in the flour and fold in. Place the egg whites in a separate, spotlessly clean bowl and whisk until soft peaks form. Gently fold the egg whites into the ricotta mixture.

2 Set a large, non-stick frying pan over a medium heat and add heaped tablespoonfuls of mixture, allowing room for them to spread. Cook for 1–2 minutes, or until the underside is coloured, then turn over with a palette knife and cook on the other side for a further 2 minutes.

3 Wrap in a clean tea towel to keep warm until all the pancakes are cooked. Serve with the warmed conserve.

buttermilk scones

makes 8   **prep: 15 mins**   **cook: 12–15 mins**

Buttermilk makes these delicious scones taste extra light and gives them an especially tangy flavour.

INGREDIENTS

55 g/2 oz cold butter, cut into pieces, plus extra for greasing

300 g/10½ oz self-raising flour, plus extra for dusting

1 tsp baking powder

pinch of salt

40 g/1½ oz golden caster sugar

300 ml/10 fl oz buttermilk

2 tbsp milk

TO SERVE

whipped cream

strawberry jam

NUTRITIONAL INFORMATION

Calories 210

Protein 5g

Carbohydrate 36g

Sugars 8g

Fat 6g

Saturates 4g

---

variation

These scones also taste delicious topped with whipped cream and sliced fresh strawberries.

---

cook's tip

Dip the cutter in a little flour to prevent it sticking to the dough when you cut out the scone rounds.

1 Preheat the oven to 220°C/425°F/Gas Mark 7, then grease a baking sheet. Sift the flour, baking powder and salt into a bowl. Add the butter and rub in until the mixture resembles fine breadcrumbs. Add the sugar and buttermilk and quickly mix together.

2 Turn the mixture out on to a floured work surface and knead lightly. Roll out to 2.5 cm/1 inch thick. Using a 6-cm/2½-inch plain or fluted cutter, stamp out scones and place on the prepared baking sheet. Gather the trimmings, re-roll and stamp out more scones until all the dough is used up.

3 Brush the tops of the scones with milk. Bake in the preheated oven for 12–15 minutes, or until well risen and golden. Transfer to a wire rack to cool. Split and serve with whipped cream and strawberry jam.

welsh cakes

makes 16   **prep: 15 mins**   **cook: 18 mins**

You do not even have to light the oven to make these little scones. They were traditionally cooked on a flat griddle over a fire, but a heavy frying pan on top of the stove works just as well!

INGREDIENTS

225 g/8 oz self-raising flour	85 g/3 oz golden caster sugar
pinch of salt	85 g/3 oz currants
55 g/2 oz white cooking fat	1 egg, beaten
55 g/2 oz butter, plus	1 tbsp milk (optional)
extra for greasing	caster sugar, for dusting

NUTRITIONAL INFORMATION

Calories	143
Protein	2g
Carbohydrate	20g
Sugars	9g
Fat	7g
Saturates	3g

variation

You can substitute raisins, sultanas or chopped glacé cherries for the currants, if you prefer.

cook's tip

Make sure that the heat under the griddle or frying pan remains low during cooking to avoid burning the surface of the cakes.

1 Sift the flour and salt into a bowl. Add the white cooking fat and butter and rub in until the mixture resembles breadcrumbs. Stir in the sugar and currants. Add the egg and a little milk, if necessary, to make a soft, but not sticky, dough.

2 On a floured work surface, roll out the dough to 5 mm/¼ inch thick. Stamp into rounds with a 6-cm/2½-inch plain or fluted cutter. Gather the trimmings, re-roll and stamp out more cakes until all the dough is used up.

3 Grease a griddle or heavy-based frying pan and set over a low heat. Cook the cakes for 3 minutes on each side, or until golden brown. Dust generously with caster sugar and serve warm or cold.

scotch pancakes with orange butter

makes 20   **prep: 15–20 mins**   **cook: 15–20 mins**

Traditional Scotch pancakes are sometimes known as drop scones, but whatever they are called, they will always be a very welcome sight on the tea table.

INGREDIENTS

225 g/8 oz self-raising flour

2 tsp baking powder

pinch of salt

25 g/1 oz golden caster sugar

1 egg

225 ml/8 fl oz milk

butter, for greasing

ORANGE BUTTER

175 g/6 oz butter

25 g/1 oz icing sugar, sifted

finely grated rind of 1 orange and

2 tbsp orange juice

NUTRITIONAL INFORMATION

Calories 124

Protein 2g

Carbohydrate 12g

Sugars 3g

Fat 8g

Saturates 5g

---

variation

As an alternative to the orange butter, serve butter and jam or honey with the pancakes.

---

cook's tip

Heat up the griddle or frying pan gently and check it is ready by dropping a small amount of pancake batter on to the surface, which should sizzle.

1 To make the orange butter, place all of the ingredients in a bowl and beat together until light and fluffy. Leave to chill in the refrigerator while making the pancakes.

2 To make the pancakes, sift the flour, baking powder and salt into a bowl. Stir in the sugar and make a well in the centre. Place the egg and milk in a separate bowl, whisk together and pour into the well. Gradually draw the flour into the liquid by stirring with a wooden spoon, then beat thoroughly to make a smooth batter.

3 Grease a griddle or heavy-based frying pan and set over a medium–high heat. Drop dessertspoonfuls of the batter into the pan and cook for 2–3 minutes, or until bubbles burst on the surface and the underside is golden. Turn over with a palette knife and cook for a further 1 minute, or until golden on the other side. Keep warm in a clean tea towel until all the pancakes are cooked. Serve with the orange butter.

bacon & polenta muffins

makes 12 **prep: 20 mins** ⏲ **cook: 20–25 mins** ⏲

These muffins are delicious served warm for breakfast or as an accompaniment to chicken or game casseroles.

INGREDIENTS

150 g/5½ oz pancetta

150 g/5½ oz self-raising flour

1 tbsp baking powder

1 tsp salt

250 g/9 oz fine polenta

55 g/2 oz golden granulated sugar

100 g/3½ oz butter, melted

2 eggs, beaten

300 ml/10 fl oz milk

NUTRITIONAL INFORMATION	
Calories	.280
Protein	.7g
Carbohydrate	.31g
Sugars	.6g
Fat	.15g
Saturates	.7g

cook's tip

Pancetta is thin Italian bacon. If it is unavailable, you can use thinly sliced rashers of streaky bacon instead.

1 Preheat the oven to 200°C/400°F/Gas Mark 6 and preheat the grill to medium. Line 12 holes of 1 or 2 muffin trays with paper muffin cases. Cook the pancetta under the preheated grill until crisp and then crumble into pieces. Reserve until required.

2 Sift the flour, baking powder and salt into a bowl, then stir in the polenta and sugar. Place the butter, eggs and milk in a separate bowl. Add the wet ingredients to the dry ingredients and mix until just blended.

3 Fold in the pancetta, then divide the mixture between the paper cases and bake in the preheated oven for 20–25 minutes, or until risen and golden. Serve the muffins warm or cold.

cheese muffins

cook: 20–25 mins   **prep: 15 mins**   **makes 10**

These savoury muffins are delicious served with soup,
turning it into a filling main meal.

NUTRITIONAL INFORMATION	
Calories	.260
Protein	.9g
Carbohydrate	.27g
Sugars	.2g
Fat	.13g
Saturates	.7g

INGREDIENTS

115 g/4 oz self-raising flour

1 tbsp baking powder

1 tsp salt

225 g/8 oz fine polenta

150 g/5½ oz grated mature
Cheddar cheese

55 g/2 oz butter, melted

2 eggs, beaten

1 garlic clove, crushed

300 ml/10 fl oz milk

cook's tip

Polenta, or cornmeal, used to
be difficult to find, but it is
now widely available in most
major supermarkets and health
food shops.

1 Preheat the oven to 200°C/400°F/Gas Mark 6. Line 10 holes of 1 or 2 muffin trays with paper muffin cases. Sift the flour, baking powder and salt into a bowl, then stir in the polenta and 115 g/4 oz of the cheese.

2 Place the melted butter, eggs, crushed garlic and milk in a separate bowl. Add the wet ingredients to the dry ingredients and mix gently until just combined.

3 Using a spoon, divide the mixture between the paper cases, scatter over the remaining cheese and bake in the preheated oven for 20–25 minutes, or until risen and golden brown. Serve warm or cold.

cheese & chive scones

makes 8   **prep: 15 mins** ⏲   **cook: 10 mins** ⏲

Savoury scones make a delicious alternative to sandwiches at tea-time and they are ideal for serving with soup.

INGREDIENTS

40 g/1½ oz butter, plus extra for greasing

115 g/4 oz white self-raising flour, plus extra for dusting

115 g/4 oz wholemeal self-raising flour

1 tsp baking powder

pinch of salt

85 g/3 oz finely grated Cheddar cheese

2 tbsp snipped fresh chives

3 tbsp milk

fresh chives, to garnish

NUTRITIONAL INFORMATION

Calories	182
Protein	6g
Carbohydrate	21g
Sugars	1g
Fat	9g
Saturates	5g

cook's tip

Choose a mature, well-flavoured Cheddar cheese for these scones, to give them a strong, well-rounded taste.

1 Preheat the oven to 220°C/425°F/Gas Mark 7, then grease a baking sheet. Sift the 2 flours, baking powder and salt into a bowl. Rub in the butter until the mixture resembles fine breadcrumbs, then stir in 55 g/2 oz of the grated cheese and chives. Stir in up to 1 tablespoon of milk to make a fairly soft, light dough.

2 On a floured work surface, roll out the dough to 2 cm/¾ inch thick and stamp into rounds with a 6-cm/2½-inch plain cutter. Gather the trimmings, re-roll and stamp out more scones until the dough is used up.

3 Place the scones on the prepared baking sheet, brush the tops with the remaining milk and sprinkle with the remaining grated cheese. Bake in the preheated oven for 10 minutes, or until well risen and golden. Garnish with fresh chives and serve warm or cold.

blinis

cook: 20 mins

prep: 20 mins, plus 1 hr standing

makes 8

Blinis are Russian yeast pancakes traditionally made with buckwheat flour, which gives them a tasty and unusual flavour.

NUTRITIONAL INFORMATION	
Calories	170
Protein	6g
Carbohydrate	25g
Sugars	3g
Fat	6g
Saturates	2g

INGREDIENTS

115 g/4 oz buckwheat flour

115 g/4 oz strong white bread flour

7-g/⅛-oz sachet easy-blend dried yeast

1 tsp salt

375 ml/13 fl oz tepid milk

2 eggs, 1 whole and 1 separated

vegetable oil, for brushing

TO SERVE

soured cream

smoked salmon

variation

If buckwheat flour is unavailable, use wholemeal bread flour instead.

1 Sift both flours into a large, warmed bowl. Stir in the yeast and salt. Beat in the milk, whole egg and egg yolk until smooth. Cover the bowl and leave to stand in a warm place for 1 hour.

2 Place the egg white in a spotlessly clean bowl and whisk until soft peaks form. Fold into the batter. Brush a heavy-based frying pan with vegetable oil and set over a medium–high heat. When the frying pan is hot, pour enough of the batter on to the surface to make a blini about the size of a saucer.

3 When bubbles rise, turn the blini over with a palette knife and cook the other side until light brown. Wrap in a clean tea towel to keep warm while cooking the remainder. Serve the warm blinis with soured cream and smoked salmon.

large cakes

You only have to look at the crowds around the cake stall at any fund-raising event to know that everyone loves a home-made cake. But no magic is required to produce a wonderful cake that will make a stunning centrepiece at any tea table. The cakes in this section are not complicated, and none of them have elaborate decoration. There are plenty of books dedicated to the art of cake decorating, so the cakes here have simple frostings, colourful fruit toppings or sticky syrup drizzled over them.

You will find a variety of cakes, from family favourites, such as Cherry & Almond Cake (see page 136) and Carrot Cake (see page 146), to wickedly rich Mississippi Mud Cake (see page 149). There are spicy cakes such as Preserved Ginger Cake (see page 134) and Honey Spice Cake (see page 141), which fill the kitchen with a fragrant aroma, and moist dessert cakes with fruit. Who could resist Blueberry & Lemon Drizzle Cake (see page 144), Passion Fruit Angel Cake (see page 150) or Pear & Cinnamon Cake (see page 140). Classic recipes have not been forgotten, and a rich, fruity Christmas Cake has been included (see page 142) along with an easy Victoria Sandwich Cake (see page 151), mixed using the all-in-one method. The beauty of this recipe is that you can make endless variations on it once you have mastered the basics.

Some of the cakes are best when freshly made, and others, such as Cherry & Almond Cake, will keep for a few days. Preserved Ginger Cake benefits from being kept for a day or two before serving, though you will probably have trouble resisting it for more than a few hours!

preserved ginger cake

serves 12

prep: 20 mins, plus 1 hr cooling

cook: 45–50 mins

Ground ginger, preserved ginger and ginger syrup make this a really gingery cake! Its rich flavour is warming and moreish.

INGREDIENTS

115 g/4 oz butter, plus extra for greasing

225 g/8 oz self-raising flour

1 tbsp ground ginger

1 tsp ground cinnamon

½ tsp bicarbonate of soda

115 g/4 oz light muscovado sugar

grated rind of ½ lemon

2 eggs

1½ tbsp golden syrup

1½ tbsp milk

TOPPING

6 pieces of stem ginger, plus 4 tbsp ginger syrup from the jar

115 g/4 oz icing sugar

lemon juice

NUTRITIONAL INFORMATION

Calories 243

Protein 3g

Carbohydrate 40g

Sugars 25g

Fat 9g

Saturates 6g

variation

If you don't want to decorate the cake with stem ginger pieces, try a layer of icing lightly sprinkled with ground cinnamon instead.

cook's tip

This cake will taste much better if it is kept in an airtight container for a day before eating, to give the ginger flavour time to develop.

1 Preheat the oven to 160°C/325°F/Gas Mark 3. Grease and line the base of an 18-cm/7-inch square tin. Sift the flour, ginger, cinnamon and bicarbonate of soda into a bowl. Rub in the butter, then stir in the sugar and lemon rind. Make a well in the centre. Place the eggs, syrup and milk in a separate bowl and whisk together. Pour into the dry ingredients and beat until smooth.

2 Spoon the mixture into the prepared tin and bake in the preheated oven for 45–50 minutes, or until well risen and firm to the touch. Leave the cake to cool in the tin for 30 minutes, then turn out on to a wire rack and peel off the lining paper. Leave to cool completely.

3 To make the topping, cut each piece of stem ginger into quarters and arrange the pieces on top of the cake. Sift the icing sugar into a bowl and stir in the ginger syrup and enough lemon juice to make a smooth icing. Place the icing in a polythene bag and cut a tiny hole in one corner. Drizzle the icing over the cake. Leave to set, then cut the cake into squares and serve.

cherry & almond cake

serves 8   **prep: 15 mins, plus** ⏲   **cook: 1 hr 30 mins–** ⏲
                    30 mins cooling   **1 hr 45 mins**

Ground almonds add richness to this cake and help its keeping qualities. It's sure to become a family favourite.

INGREDIENTS

175 g/6 oz butter, softened, plus extra for greasing

225 g/8 oz glacé cherries

175 g/6 oz golden caster sugar

3 eggs

55 g/2 oz ground almonds

225 g/8 oz plain flour

1½ tsp baking powder

40 g/1½ oz flaked almonds

NUTRITIONAL INFORMATION

Calories 518

Protein 8g

Carbohydrate 65g

Sugars 43g

Fat 27g

Saturates 13g

variation

You can substitute chopped no-soak apricots for the glacé cherries in this cake, if you prefer.

cook's tip

Washing and drying the glacé cherries before using them in the recipe helps prevent them sinking to the bottom of the cake.

1 Preheat the oven to 160°C/325°F/Gas Mark 3. Grease and line the base of an 18-cm/7-inch deep cake tin. Cut the cherries in half, then place them in a sieve and rinse to remove all the syrup. Pat dry with kitchen paper and reserve.

2 Place the butter, caster sugar, eggs and ground almonds in a bowl. Sift in the flour and baking powder. Beat thoroughly until smooth, then stir in the cherries. Spoon the mixture into the prepared tin and smooth the top.

3 Sprinkle the flaked almonds over the cake. Bake in the preheated oven for 1½–1¾ hours, or until well risen and a skewer inserted into the centre of the cake comes out clean. Leave to cool in the tin for 10 minutes, then turn out on to a wire rack, remove the lining paper and leave to cool.

caribbean coconut cake

serves 8

prep: 20 mins, plus 30 mins cooling

cook: 25 mins

Desiccated coconut and coconut cream make this moist cake rich and delicious, and are perfectly complemented by pineapple jam.

INGREDIENTS

280 g/10 oz butter, softened, plus extra for greasing

175 g/6 oz golden caster sugar

3 eggs

175 g/6 oz self-raising flour

1½ tsp baking powder

½ tsp freshly grated nutmeg

55 g/2 oz desiccated coconut

5 tbsp coconut cream

280 g/10 oz icing sugar

5 tbsp pineapple jam

toasted shredded coconut, to decorate

NUTRITIONAL INFORMATION

Calories	.694
Protein	.6g
Carbohydrate	.84g
Sugars	.68g
Fat	.40g
Saturates	.27g

cook's tip

Coconut cream comes in small cartons. What remains after making this cake can be used in custards, soups or curries, or can be poured over fresh fruit in place of cream.

1 Preheat the oven to 180°C/350°F/Gas Mark 4. Grease and line the bases of 2 x 20-cm/8-inch sandwich tins. Place 175 g/6 oz of the butter in a bowl with the sugar and eggs and sift in the flour, baking powder and nutmeg. Beat together until smooth, then stir in the coconut and 2 tablespoons of the coconut cream.

2 Divide the mixture between the prepared tins and smooth the tops. Bake in the preheated oven for 25 minutes, or until golden and firm to the touch. Leave to cool in the tins for 5 minutes, then turn out on to a wire rack, peel off the lining paper and leave to cool completely.

3 Sift the icing sugar into a bowl and add the remaining butter and coconut cream. Beat together until smooth. Spread the pineapple jam on one of the cakes and top with just under half of the buttercream. Place the other cake on top. Spread the remaining buttercream on top of the cake and scatter with toasted shredded coconut.

jewel-topped madeira cake

⏲ **cook: 1 hr 15 mins– 1 hr 30 mins**   ⏱ **prep: 25 mins, plus 30 mins cooling**   **serves 8**

Brightly coloured crystallized fruits make a stunning and unusual topping for this classic Madeira cake.

NUTRITIONAL INFORMATION	
Calories	.570
Protein	.7g
Carbohydrate	.81g
Sugars	.55g
Fat	.27g
Saturates	.16g

INGREDIENTS

225 g/8 oz butter, softened, plus extra for greasing

225 g/8 oz golden caster sugar

finely grated rind of 1 lemon

4 eggs, beaten

280 g/10 oz self-raising flour, sifted

2–3 tbsp milk

FRUIT TOPPING

2½ tbsp clear honey

225 g/8 oz crystallized fruit

variation

Traditionally, a Madeira cake is simply decorated with a slice of candied peel on top, which is placed on the cake after it has been cooking for 1 hour.

1 Preheat the oven to 160°C/325°F/Gas Mark 3. Grease and line the base of a deep 20-cm/8-inch round cake tin. Place the butter, sugar and lemon rind in a bowl and beat together until light and fluffy. Gradually beat in the eggs. Gently fold in the flour, alternating with enough milk to give a soft, dropping consistency.

2 Spoon the mixture into the prepared tin and bake in the preheated oven for 1¼–1½ hours, or until risen and golden and a skewer inserted into the centre comes out clean.

3 Leave to cool in the tin for 10 minutes, then turn out on to a wire rack and remove the lining paper. Leave to cool completely. To make the topping, brush the honey over the cake and arrange the fruit on top.

pear & cinnamon cake

serves 8 | **prep: 20 mins, plus 30 mins cooling** | **cook: 55–60 mins**

This cake smells wonderful while it is baking, and is a delicious way to end a memorable meal.

INGREDIENTS

3–4 firm pears, depending on the size

1 vanilla pod

200 g/7 oz butter, melted and cooled, plus extra for greasing

275 g/9½ oz golden caster sugar

2 large eggs

250 g/9 oz plain flour

1 tbsp ground cinnamon

½ tsp bicarbonate of soda

4 tbsp golden icing sugar

NUTRITIONAL INFORMATION	
Calories	.508
Protein	.5g
Carbohydrate	.76g
Sugars	.52g
Fat	.23g
Saturates	.14g

variation

As an alternative to fresh pears, canned pears will work almost as well.

1 Peel and quarter the pears and remove the cores. Cut the pears into small cubes, place in a saucepan and cover with water. Split the vanilla pod to expose the seeds, and add to the saucepan. Bring to the boil, then reduce the heat and simmer gently until the pears are tender. Remove from the heat and leave to cool. Preheat the oven to 180°C/350°F/Gas Mark 4. Thoroughly grease and line the base of a 20-cm/8-inch springform cake tin. Drain the pears, reserving their cooking liquid, and pat dry with kitchen paper.

2 Place the sugar, eggs and butter in a bowl and whisk together. Sift the flour, cinnamon and bicarbonate of soda into a separate bowl. Fold the flour mixture into the sugar and egg mixture, one-third at a time. Fold in the pears.

3 Transfer the mixture to the prepared tin and bake in the preheated oven for 50–55 minutes, or until a skewer inserted into the centre comes out clean. Leave to cool in the tin for 20 minutes, then turn out on to a wire rack, peel off the lining paper and leave to cool.

4 Sift the icing sugar into a bowl and add enough of the reserved pear cooking liquid to give a pouring consistency. Drizzle the icing over the cake and leave to set before serving.

honey spice cake

⏱ **cook: 45–55 mins**   ⏲ **prep: 15 mins, plus 30 mins cooling**   **serves 8**

This cake can be made in advance, as it benefits from being kept for a day before eating to let the flavours develop.

NUTRITIONAL INFORMATION	
Calories	.534
Protein	.4g
Carbohydrate	.97g
Sugars	.78g
Fat	.17g
Saturates	.11g

INGREDIENTS

150 g/5½ oz butter, plus

extra for greasing

115 g/4 oz light muscovado sugar

175 g/6 oz clear honey

1 tbsp water

200 g/7 oz self-raising flour

½ tsp ground ginger

½ tsp ground cinnamon

½ tsp caraway seeds

seeds from 8 cardamom pods, ground

2 eggs, beaten

350 g/12 oz icing sugar

cook's tip

Try to choose a strongly flavoured honey so that its richness is not totally overpowered by the flavours of all the spices.

1 Preheat the oven to 180°C/350°F/Gas Mark 4. Grease an 850-ml/1½-pint fluted cake tin. Place the butter, sugar, honey and water into a heavy-based saucepan. Set over a low heat and stir until the butter has melted and the sugar has dissolved. Remove from the heat and leave to cool for 10 minutes.

2 Sift the flour into a bowl and mix in the ginger, cinnamon, caraway seeds and cardamom. Make a well in the centre. Pour in the honey mixture and the eggs and beat well until smooth. Pour the batter into the prepared tin and bake in the preheated oven for 40–50 minutes, or until well risen and a skewer inserted into the centre comes out clean. Leave to cool in the tin for 5 minutes, then transfer to a wire rack to cool completely.

3 Sift the icing sugar into a bowl. Stir in enough warm water to make a smooth, flowing icing. Spoon over the cake, allowing it to flow down the sides, then leave to set.

christmas cake

serves 32

prep: 15 mins, plus 20 mins cooling

cook: 3 hrs 10 mins– 3 hrs 40 mins

This is an easy way of making a Christmas cake, as no creaming or careful folding-in is required. Boiling the fruit mixture first makes the cake taste especially moist and flavoursome.

INGREDIENTS

250 g/9 oz butter, cut into pieces, plus extra for greasing

300 g/10½ oz dark muscovado sugar

2 tbsp black treacle

1.5 kg/3 lb 5 oz luxury dried fruit

finely grated rind and juice of 1 large orange

90 ml/3¼ fl oz brandy

5 eggs, beaten

175 g/6 oz mixed nuts, roughly chopped

55 g/2 oz ground almonds

325 g/11½ oz plain flour

½ tsp baking powder

1 tbsp ground mixed spice

NUTRITIONAL INFORMATION

Calories 330

Protein 5g

Carbohydrate 52g

Sugars 44g

Fat 12g

Saturates 5g

variation

You could substitute rum for the brandy, if you would prefer a slightly different taste to this rich fruit cake.

cook's tip

Cover the cake with marzipan and icing. Alternatively, you can simply top the cake with an arrangement of luxury nuts and dried fruit.

1 Place the butter, sugar, treacle, dried fruit, orange rind and juice and brandy in a large saucepan. Bring slowly to the boil, then reduce the heat and simmer gently for 10 minutes, stirring occasionally. Remove from the heat and leave to cool.

2 Preheat the oven to 150°C/300°F/Gas Mark 2. Grease and line the base of a deep 20-cm/8-inch round cake tin and wrap a double layer of paper around the outside of the tin. Stir the eggs, mixed nuts and ground almonds into the cooled fruit mixture and mix well. Sift in the flour, baking powder and mixed spice. Stir in gently but thoroughly. Spoon into the prepared tin. Smooth the top.

3 Bake in the preheated oven for 1 hour, then reduce the heat to 140°C/275°F/Gas Mark 1 and bake for 2–2½ hours, or until a skewer inserted into the centre comes out clean. Leave to cool in the tin, then turn out and store, wrapped in greaseproof paper and foil, until ready to decorate.

blueberry & lemon drizzle cake

serves 12

prep: 20 mins, plus 30 mins cooling

cook: 1 hr

The lemon syrup that is poured over this cake gives it a wonderful fresh, tangy flavour – a perfect complement to the blueberries.

INGREDIENTS

225 g/8 oz butter, softened, plus extra for greasing

225 g/8 oz golden caster sugar

4 eggs, beaten

250 g/9 oz self-raising flour, sifted

finely grated rind and juice of 1 lemon

25 g/1 oz ground almonds

200 g/7 oz fresh blueberries

TOPPING

juice of 2 lemons

115 g/4 oz golden caster sugar

NUTRITIONAL INFORMATION

Calories	.364
Protein	.5g
Carbohydrate	.47g
Sugars	.31g
Fat	.19g
Saturates	.11g

cook's tip

If you warm a lemon gently in the microwave for a few seconds on High, it will yield more juice when you squeeze it.

1 Preheat the oven to 180°C/350°F/Gas Mark 4, then grease and line the base of a 20-cm/8-inch square cake tin. Place the butter and sugar in a bowl and beat together until light and fluffy. Gradually beat in the eggs, adding a little flour towards the end to prevent curdling. Beat in the lemon rind, then fold in the remaining flour and almonds with enough of the lemon juice to give a good dropping consistency.

2 Fold in three-quarters of the blueberries and turn into the prepared tin. Smooth the surface, then scatter the remaining blueberries on top. Bake in the preheated oven for 1 hour, or until firm to the touch and a skewer inserted into the centre comes out clean.

3 To make the topping, place the lemon juice and sugar in a bowl and mix together. As soon as the cake comes out of the oven, prick it all over with a fine skewer and pour over the lemon mixture. Leave to cool in the tin until completely cold, then cut into 12 squares to serve.

sticky date cake

 cook: 1 hr 10 mins– 1 hr 25 mins

prep: 20 mins, plus 30 mins cooling

serves 8

The toffee topping on this cake makes it very moreish. It can be a comforting or sophisticated dessert, depending on its presentation.

NUTRITIONAL INFORMATION

Calories 534

Protein 6g

Carbohydrate 75g

Sugars 54g

Fat 25g

Saturates 16g

INGREDIENTS

225 g/8 oz stoned dates, chopped

300 ml/10 fl oz boiling water

115 g/4 oz butter, softened, plus extra for greasing

175 g/6 oz golden caster sugar

3 eggs, beaten

225 g/8 oz self-raising flour, sifted

½ tsp ground cinnamon

1 tsp bicarbonate of soda

TOPPING

85 g/3 oz light muscovado sugar

55 g/2 oz butter

3 tbsp double cream

cook's tip

Soaking dates for a few minutes in boiling water restores their moisture and gives them a delicious toffee-like consistency ideal for cakes and desserts.

1 Place the dates in a bowl and cover them with the boiling water. Preheat the oven to 180°C/ 350°F/Gas Mark 4, then grease a 23-cm/9-inch springform cake tin. Place the butter and sugar in a bowl and beat until light and fluffy. Gradually beat in the eggs, then fold in the flour and cinnamon.

2 Add the bicarbonate of soda to the dates and water, then pour on to the creamed mixture. Stir until well mixed. Pour into the prepared tin and bake in the oven for 1–1¼ hours, or until well risen and firm to the touch.

3 Preheat the grill to medium. To make the topping, place the sugar, butter and cream in a saucepan. Set over a low heat, stirring, until the sugar has melted, then bring to the boil and simmer for 3 minutes. Pour over the cake and place the cake under the preheated grill until the topping is bubbling. Leave to cool in the tin until the topping has set, then transfer to a wire rack to cool completely before serving.

carrot cake

serves 8　　　　　**prep: 15 mins, plus** ⏲　　　**cook: 1 hr 5 mins** ♨
20 mins cooling/standing

Carrots give this cake a surprisingly sweet, wholesome
flavour and an attractive golden colour.

INGREDIENTS

butter, for greasing

175 g/6 oz light muscovado sugar

3 eggs

175 ml/6 fl oz sunflower oil

175 g/6 oz coarsely grated carrots

2 ripe bananas, mashed

55 g/2 oz walnuts, chopped

280 g/10 oz plain flour

½ tsp salt

1 tsp bicarbonate of soda

2 tsp baking powder

FROSTING

200 g/7 oz cream cheese

½ tsp vanilla essence

115 g/4 oz icing sugar

25 g/1 oz walnuts, chopped

NUTRITIONAL INFORMATION

Calories 650

Protein 9g

Carbohydrate 73g

Sugars 46g

Fat 38g

Saturates 11g

---

variation

If you prefer, you can bake the
mixture in a rectangular tin and cut
the finished cake into squares.

cook's tip

The more coarsely you
grate the carrots, the more
texture this cake will have.
If you prefer a smoother
texture, grate the carrots a
little more finely.

1 Preheat the oven
to 180°C/350°F/Gas
Mark 4. Grease and line the
base of a 23-cm/9-inch
springform cake tin. Place the
sugar, eggs, sunflower oil,
carrots, bananas and walnuts
in a bowl. Sift in the flour, salt,
bicarbonate of soda and
baking powder. Beat the
mixture until smooth.

2 Turn the mixture into
the prepared tin and
bake in the preheated oven for
1 hour 5 minutes, or until well
risen and golden brown and a
skewer inserted into the centre
comes out clean. Leave in the
tin for 10 minutes, then turn
out and peel off the lining
paper. Transfer to a wire rack
to cool completely.

3 To make the frosting,
place the cream cheese
and vanilla essence in a bowl
and beat well to soften. Beat
in the icing sugar a tablespoon
at a time, until smooth. Swirl
over the cake and sprinkle the
chopped walnuts on top. Leave
in a cool place for the frosting
to harden slightly before
serving.

coffee caramel cake

serves 8   **prep: 20 mins, plus**   **cook: 35 mins**
20 mins cooling

*This intensely flavoured coffee cake is complemented perfectly
by a soft and deliciously sweet caramel icing.*

INGREDIENTS

175 g/6 oz butter, softened,
plus extra for greasing
175 g/6 oz golden caster sugar
3 eggs, beaten
225 g/8 oz self-raising flour, sifted
100 ml/3½ fl oz strong black coffee
chocolate-covered coffee beans,
to decorate

ICING

125 ml/4 fl oz milk
125 g/4½ oz butter
3 tbsp golden caster sugar
575 g/1 lb 4½ oz icing sugar

NUTRITIONAL INFORMATION	
Calories 518
Protein 6g
Carbohydrate 51g
Sugars 30g
Fat 34g
Saturates 21g

cook's tip

Take extra care when adding
the warm milk mixture to the
caramel in Step 2, because
the hot liquid may splutter
and burn.

1 Preheat the oven
to 180°C/350°F/Gas
Mark 4, then grease and line
the base of 2 x 20-cm/8-inch
sandwich tins. Place the butter
and sugar in a bowl and beat
together until light and fluffy.
Gradually beat in the eggs,
then fold in the flour and
coffee. Divide the mixture
between the prepared tins and
bake in the preheated oven for

30 minutes, or until well risen
and springy when pressed in
the centre. Leave to cool in the
tins for 5 minutes, then turn
out and peel off the lining
paper. Transfer to wire racks
to cool completely.

2 To make the icing,
place the milk and
butter in a saucepan, set over
a low heat and stir until the

butter has melted. Remove the
saucepan from the heat and
reserve. Place the caster sugar
in a separate, heavy-based
saucepan and set over a low
heat, stirring constantly, until
the sugar dissolves and turns
a golden caramel. Remove
from the heat and stir in the
warm milk mixture. Return to
the heat and stir until the
caramel dissolves.

3 Remove from the heat
and gradually stir in the
icing sugar, beating until the
icing is a smooth spreading
consistency. Sandwich the
cakes together with some of
the icing and spread the rest
over the top and sides.
Decorate with chocolate-
covered coffee beans.

mississippi mud cake

cook: 1 hr 30 mins   **prep: 25 mins, plus 30 mins cooling**   **serves 16**

Mud cake is a rich, dense chocolate cake that can be served with crème fraîche or fresh berries, or plain with after-dinner coffee.

NUTRITIONAL INFORMATION

Calories	.344
Protein	.3g
Carbohydrate	.46g
Sugars	.34g
Fat	.17g
Saturates	.11g

INGREDIENTS

250 g/9 oz butter, cut into pieces, plus extra for greasing

150 g/5½ oz plain chocolate

425 g/15 oz golden caster sugar

250 ml/9 fl oz hot water

3 tbsp Tia Maria or brandy

250 g/9 oz plain flour

1 tsp baking powder

25 g/1 oz cocoa powder

2 eggs, beaten

TO DECORATE

fresh raspberries

chocolate curls

cook's tip

If the cake begins to brown too quickly while baking, cover the top loosely with a piece of foil for the remainder of the cooking time.

1 Preheat the oven to 160°C/325°F/Gas Mark 3, then grease and line a 20-cm/8-inch round cake tin. Break the chocolate into pieces, then place the butter, chocolate, sugar, hot water and Tia Maria in a large, heavy-based saucepan over a low heat and stir until the chocolate melts.

2 Stir until smooth, transfer the mixture to a large bowl and leave to cool for 15 minutes. Sift in the flour, baking powder and cocoa and whisk in, then whisk in the eggs. Pour the mixture into the prepared cake tin.

3 Bake in the preheated oven for 1½ hours, or until risen and firm to the touch. Leave to cool in the tin for 30 minutes, then turn out and peel off the lining paper. Transfer to a wire rack to cool completely. Decorate with fresh raspberries and chocolate curls and serve.

passion fruit angel cake

serves 8   **prep: 20 mins, plus** 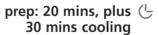   **cook: 50–55 mins**
30 mins cooling

This American angel cake is wonderfully light and airy, and its unusual and delicious passion fruit icing is bound to be a talking point among your guests.

INGREDIENTS

85 g/3 oz plain flour

280 g/10 oz caster sugar

8 large egg whites

1 tsp cream of tartar

pinch of salt

1 tsp vanilla essence

2 tbsp warm water

ICING

4 passion fruit

200 g/7 oz icing sugar

NUTRITIONAL INFORMATION

Calories	.288
Protein	.4g
Carbohydrate	.72g
Sugars	.64g
Fat	.0g
Saturates	.0g

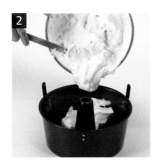

1   Preheat the oven to 180°C/350°F/Gas Mark 4. Sift the flour and 2 tablespoons of the sugar on to a sheet of greaseproof paper. Place the egg whites in a large, spotlessly clean bowl and whisk until frothy, then stir in the cream of tartar and salt. Sprinkle in the vanilla essence and warm water and continue whisking until the egg whites are stiff but not dry. Sift in the remaining sugar, 2 tablespoons at a time, whisking well between each addition, until soft peaks form.

2   Gently fold in the sifted flour and sugar mixture, in several batches. Pour the mixture into a non-stick angel cake tin with a funnel. It should be about two-thirds full. Bake in the preheated oven for 50–55 minutes, or until the top is brown and dry to the touch. Turn the tin upside down and leave until the cake is completely cold. Using a palette knife, ease the cake out of the tin and transfer to a serving plate.

3   To make the icing, cut the passion fruit in half and scoop out the pulp into a sieve set over a bowl. Press the juice from the pulp with a wooden spoon. Stir enough icing sugar into the juice to make an icing with the consistency of double cream. Drizzle the icing over the cake and leave to set.

cook's tip

If you do not have an angel cake tin, any other type of cake tin, such as an ungreased tube tin, can be used as a substitute.

victoria sandwich cake

cook: 25–30 mins   **prep: 10 mins, plus 20 mins cooling**   **serves 8**

A Victoria sandwich cake is probably the first cake that most people learn to make and it is usually made by the creaming method, but this is a quicker way, using the all-in-one method.

NUTRITIONAL INFORMATION

Calories 720

Protein 6g

Carbohydrate 51g

Sugars 35g

Fat 56g

Saturates 35g

INGREDIENTS

175 g/6 oz butter, softened,
plus extra for greasing

175 g/6 oz self-raising flour

1 tsp baking powder

175 g/6 oz golden caster sugar

3 eggs

FILLING

3 tbsp raspberry jam

600 ml/1 pint double cream, whipped

16 fresh strawberries, halved

caster sugar, for dusting

variations

Sandwich the cakes with lemon curd or another fruit jam and fresh fruit.

1 Preheat the oven to 180°C/350°F/Gas Mark 4, then grease and line the bases of 2 x 20-cm/8-inch sandwich tins. Sift the flour and baking powder into a bowl and add the butter, sugar and eggs. Mix together, then beat well until smooth.

2 Divide the mixture evenly between the prepared tins and smooth the surfaces. Bake in the preheated oven for 25–30 minutes, or until well risen and golden brown, and the cakes feel springy when lightly pressed.

3 Leave to cool in the tins for 5 minutes, then turn out and peel off the lining paper. Transfer to wire racks to cool completely. Sandwich the cakes together with the raspberry jam, whipped double cream and strawberry halves. Sprinkle the caster sugar on top and serve.

tropical fruit cake

serves 16   **prep: 25 mins, plus** ⏲ **9 hrs soaking/cooling**   **cook: 2 hrs 30 mins** ⏲

This is the perfect fruit cake to have in the cake tin for any occasion, but it also makes a delicious, slightly lighter alternative to the traditional, rich fruit Christmas cake.

INGREDIENTS

650 g/1 lb 7 oz mixed dried tropical fruit

115 g/4 oz no-soak dried apricots

115 g/4 oz sultanas

90 ml/3¼ fl oz rum

200 g/7 oz butter, softened, plus extra for greasing

200 g/7 oz golden caster sugar

3 eggs, beaten

200 g/7 oz plain flour

1 tsp baking powder

1 tsp ground ginger

40 g/1½ oz desiccated coconut

85 g/3 oz Brazil nuts, roughly chopped

85 g/3 oz cashew nuts, roughly chopped

25 g/1 oz stem ginger, finely chopped

NUTRITIONAL INFORMATION

Calories 413

Protein 6g

Carbohydrate 55g

Sugars 43g

Fat 19g

Saturates 9g

variation

Substitute different nuts, such as pecan nuts and walnuts, for the Brazil nuts and cashews, if you prefer.

cook's tip

You may be able to find packets of mixed dried tropical fruit. If not, choose a mixture of fruit such as mango, pineapple and pawpaw.

1 Place 400 g/14 oz of the mixed tropical fruit in a food processor with the apricots and process until chopped into small pieces. Transfer to a bowl and add the sultanas and rum. Cover and leave to soak for 8 hours, or overnight.

2 Preheat the oven to 150°C/300°F/Gas Mark 2. Grease and line the base of a deep 20-cm/8-inch round cake tin. Place the butter and sugar in a bowl and and beat together until light and fluffy, then gradually beat in the eggs, adding a little flour towards the end to prevent curdling. Sift in the remaining flour, baking powder and ground ginger and fold in. Stir in the coconut, two-thirds of the nuts, the stem ginger and the soaked fruit. Turn into the prepared tin and smooth the surface.

3 Place the remaining tropical fruit in a food processor and process until roughly chopped. Scatter over the cake with the remaining nuts. Place the cake in the preheated oven and reduce the temperature to 140°C/275°F/Gas Mark 1. Bake for 2½ hours, or until firm to the touch and a skewer inserted into the centre comes out clean. Leave to cool in the tin for 30 minutes, then turn out and peel off the lining paper. Transfer to a wire rack to cool completely.

gâteaux & puddings

As we no longer eat puddings every day, they have become something of a treat. When you produce a home-made pudding at the end of a meal, it is guaranteed to be met with cries of delight. Your friends and family will really appreciate it when you go to the trouble of making a special pudding.

There are puddings here for every occasion, whether it is a family meal or an elegant dinner party. The recipes in this section range from a stunning Mango & Passion Fruit Pavlova (see page 162) and a rich Manhattan Cheesecake (see page 160) to more homely and comforting puddings, such as Apple & Blackberry Crumble (see page 172) or a magical Lemon Puddle Pudding (see page 169) that makes its own sauce as it cooks.

There are recipes for steamed puddings, but they are not the rib-sticking, stodgy affairs you may remember from school days. Ginger & Lemon Puddings (see page 170) and Sticky Coffee & Walnut Puddings (see page 166) are light and moist. Some old favourites have been given a new twist – upside-down pudding has a new look with a tropical fruit topping (see page 167) and bread and butter pudding, made with Italian panettone, is lifted into a gourmet class (see page 168). Recipes such as Moroccan Orange & Almond Cake (see page 156) or Apple Streusel Cake (see page 158) can be served as cakes as well as desserts. When you produce any of these cakes and puddings, diets are guaranteed to be forgotten.

moroccan orange & almond cake

serves 8   **prep: 20 mins, plus** ⏲   **cook: 45–50 mins** ⏱
40 mins cooling/standing

*This moist almond cake, a rich and unusual treat, is soaked
in a fragrant orange and cardamom syrup.*

INGREDIENTS

115 g/4 oz butter, softened,
plus extra for greasing

1 orange

115 g/4 oz golden caster sugar

2 eggs, beaten

175 g/6 oz semolina

100 g/3½ oz ground almonds

1½ tsp baking powder

icing sugar, for dusting

Greek yogurt, to serve

SYRUP

300 ml/10 fl oz orange juice

130 g/4¾ oz caster sugar

8 cardamom pods, crushed

variation

If you like, you can sprinkle a few
flaked almonds over the surface of the
cake before dusting it with icing sugar.

cook's tip

Do not be tempted to rush
this cake – make sure that
you give the orange syrup
plenty of time to soak into
the sponge.

1 Preheat the oven
to 180°C/350°F/Gas
Mark 4. Grease and line the
base of a 20-cm/8-inch cake
tin. Grate the rind from the
orange, reserving some for the
decoration, and squeeze the
juice from one half. Place the
butter, orange rind and caster
sugar in a bowl and beat
together until light and fluffy.
Gradually beat in the eggs. In

a separate bowl, mix the
semolina, ground almonds and
baking powder, then fold into
the creamed mixture with the
orange juice. Spoon the
mixture into the prepared tin
and bake in the preheated
oven for 30–40 minutes, or
until well risen and a skewer
inserted into the centre comes
out clean. Leave to cool in the
tin for 10 minutes.

2 To make the syrup,
place the orange juice,
sugar and cardamom pods in
a saucepan over a low heat
and stir until the sugar has
dissolved. Bring to the boil
and simmer for 4 minutes,
or until syrupy.

3 Turn the cake out into a
deep serving dish. Using
a skewer, make holes over the

surface of the warm cake. Sieve
the syrup into a separate bowl
and spoon three-quarters of it
over the cake, then leave for
30 minutes. Dust the cake with
icing sugar and cut into slices.
Serve with the remaining syrup
drizzled around, accompanied
by Greek yogurt decorated
with the reserved orange rind.

apple streusel cake

serves 8   **prep: 20 mins, plus 40 mins cooling**   **cook: 1 hr**

This is a cross between a cake and an apple crumble and can be served either as a dessert or as a cake.

INGREDIENTS

115 g/4 oz butter, plus extra for greasing
450 g/1 lb cooking apples
175 g/6 oz self-raising flour
1 tsp ground cinnamon
pinch of salt
115 g/4 oz golden caster sugar

2 eggs
1–2 tbsp milk
icing sugar, for dusting

STREUSEL TOPPING
115 g/4 oz self-raising flour
85 g/3 oz butter
85 g/3 oz golden caster sugar

NUTRITIONAL INFORMATION

Calories 440

Protein 5g

Carbohydrate 58g

Sugars 31g

Fat 23g

Saturates 14g

variation

As an alternative to apples, you can substitute fresh rhubarb, gooseberries or pears, if you prefer.

cook's tip

Try to work quickly when you make the cake mixture in Step 2, so the sliced apples do not have time to turn brown when exposed to the air.

1 Preheat the oven to 180°C/350°F/Gas Mark 4, then grease a 23-cm/ 9-inch springform cake tin. To make the streusel topping, sift the flour into a bowl and rub in the butter until the mixture resembles coarse crumbs. Stir in the sugar and reserve.

2 Peel, core and thinly slice the apples. To make the cake, sift the flour into a bowl with the cinnamon and salt. Place the butter and sugar in a separate bowl and beat together until light and fluffy. Gradually beat in the eggs, adding a little of the flour mixture with the last addition of egg. Gently fold in half the remaining flour mixture, then fold in the rest with the milk.

3 Spoon the mixture into the prepared tin and smooth the top. Cover with the sliced apples and sprinkle the streusel topping evenly over the top. Bake in the preheated oven for 1 hour, or until browned and firm to the touch. Leave to cool in the tin before opening the sides. Dust the cake with icing sugar before serving.

manhattan cheesecake

serves 8–10 **prep: 20 mins, plus** ⟳ **cook: 35 mins** ♨
10 hrs cooling/chilling

This is a classic, American-baked cheesecake, given a splash of colour with a traditional fruity blueberry topping.

INGREDIENTS

sunflower oil, for brushing

85 g/3 oz butter

200 g/7 oz digestive biscuits, crushed

400 g/14 oz cream cheese

2 large eggs

140 g/5 oz caster sugar

1½ tsp vanilla essence

450 ml/16 fl oz soured cream

BLUEBERRY TOPPING

55 g/2 oz caster sugar

4 tbsp water

250 g/9 oz fresh blueberries

1 tsp arrowroot

NUTRITIONAL INFORMATION

Calories 658

Protein 7g

Carbohydrate 48g

Sugars 33g

Fat 50g

Saturates 30g

variation

As an alternative to blueberries, try raspberries, blackcurrants or cranberries for the topping.

cook's tip

If possible, it is best to leave the cheesecake to chill in the refrigerator overnight at the end of Step 2.

1 Preheat the oven to 190°C/375°F/Gas Mark 5. Brush a 20-cm/8-inch springform tin with oil. Melt the butter in a saucepan over a low heat. Stir in the biscuits, then spread in the tin. Place the cream cheese, eggs, 100 g/3½ oz of the sugar and ½ teaspoon of the vanilla essence in a food processor. Process until smooth. Pour over the biscuit base and smooth the top. Place on a baking tray and bake for 20 minutes, or until set. Remove from the oven and leave to stand for 20 minutes. Leave the oven switched on.

2 Mix the cream with the remaining sugar and vanilla essence in a bowl. Spoon over the cheesecake.

Return it to the oven for 10 minutes, leave to cool, then chill in the refrigerator for 8 hours or overnight.

3 To make the topping, place the sugar in a saucepan with half of the water over a low heat and stir until the sugar has dissolved. Increase the heat, add the blueberries, cover and cook for a few minutes, or until they begin to soften. Remove from the heat. Mix the arrowroot and remaining water in a bowl, add to the fruit and stir until smooth. Return to a low heat. Cook until the juice thickens and turns translucent. Leave to cool. Remove the cheesecake from the tin 1 hour before serving. Spoon the fruit on top and chill until ready to serve.

mango & passion fruit pavlova

serves 8   **prep: 30 mins, plus 1 hour cooling**   **cook: 1 hr 15 mins– 1 hr 30 mins**

The pavlova is sometimes described as Australia's national dish. It is claimed to have been invented in 1935 by an Australian chef who named it after the Russian ballerina, Anna Pavlova.

INGREDIENTS

3 egg whites

175 g/6 oz caster sugar

1 tsp cornflour, sifted

1 tsp white wine vinegar

½ tsp vanilla essence

FILLING

300 ml/10 fl oz double cream

2 mangoes

4 passion fruit

NUTRITIONAL INFORMATION	
Calories	285
Protein	2g
Carbohydrate	30g
Sugars	30g
Fat	18g
Saturates	11g

variation

Vary the fruit used in the topping according to what is available. In the summer, raspberries, strawberries and redcurrants make a stunning topping.

1 Preheat the oven to 120°C/250°F/Gas Mark ½. Line a baking sheet with non-stick baking paper and draw a 23-cm/9-inch circle on the paper. Turn the paper over. Place the egg whites in a spotlessly clean bowl and whisk until stiff. Whisk in the sugar, one-third at a time, whisking well between each addition until stiff and glossy. Fold in the cornflour, vinegar and vanilla essence.

2 Pile the meringue on to the marked circle and make a hollow in the centre. Bake in the preheated oven for 1¼–1½ hours, or until lightly coloured and dry, but a little soft in the centre. Turn off the oven and leave the meringue in the oven until cold. Peel off the baking paper. Do not worry if the meringue crumbles slightly at this stage.

3 To make the filling, place the cream in a bowl and whip until thick, then spoon on top of the pavlova. Cut the mangoes in half and slice the flesh into cubes. Pile the cubes on top of the cream. Cut the passion fruit in half and scoop out the flesh on top of the mango. Serve the pavlova immediately.

strawberry & almond roulade

⏱ **cook: 15 mins**   ⏱ **prep: 20 mins, plus 30 mins cooling**   **serves 8**

A light, flourless almond sponge is wrapped round a filling of strawberries and mascarpone cheese in this variation on a classic, popular dessert.

NUTRITIONAL INFORMATION	
Calories	.460
Protein	.11g
Carbohydrate	.33g
Sugars	.32g
Fat	.33g
Saturates	.13g

INGREDIENTS

butter, for greasing

6 eggs

200 g/7 oz golden caster sugar

2 tsp baking powder

175 g/6 oz ground almonds

icing sugar, for dusting

FILLING

150 g/5½ oz mascarpone cheese

150 ml/5 fl oz double cream

450 g/1 lb fresh strawberries

variation

Raspberries will also complement the flavour of almonds, and make a good alternative to strawberries.

1 Preheat the oven to 180°C/350°F/Gas Mark 4. Grease and line the base and sides of a 38 x 25cm/ 15 x 10-inch Swiss roll tin. Separate the eggs, placing the whites in a large bowl and the yolks in a separate bowl. Add the sugar to the yolks and whisk together until pale and thick. Place the baking powder and ground almonds in a bowl and mix together. Stir gently into the yolk mixture, taking care not to overmix. Carefully fold in the egg whites.

2 Spread in the tin and bake in the preheated oven for 15 minutes, or until firm. Cover with a clean tea towel and leave to cool in the tin. To make the filling, place the mascarpone cheese and cream in a bowl and stir together to give a spreading consistency. Place half the strawberries in a separate bowl and mash. Roughly chop the remainder and reserve. Stir the mashed strawberries into the cream.

3 Place a sheet of greaseproof paper on the work surface and dust thickly with icing sugar. Turn the roulade out on to the paper and peel off the lining paper. Spread the cream over the roulade and scatter the chopped strawberries over. Roll up and serve, cut into slices, within 1–2 hours of assembling.

peach melba meringue roulade

serves 8   **prep: 25 mins, plus 15 mins cooling**   **cook: 45–50 mins**

This cloud of meringue is a dessert to die for – crunchy on the outside and gooey within. The meringue can be made up to 8 hours before being filled, and once assembled, the roulade will keep for up to 2 days in the refrigerator.

INGREDIENTS

sunflower oil, for brushing

COULIS

350 g/12 oz fresh raspberries

115 g/4 oz icing sugar

MERINGUE

2 tsp cornflour

300 g/10½ oz caster sugar

5 large egg whites

1 tsp cider vinegar

FILLING

3 peaches, peeled, stoned and chopped (see Cook's Tip)

250 g/9 oz fresh raspberries

200 ml/7 fl oz crème fraîche

150 ml/5 fl oz double cream

NUTRITIONAL INFORMATION

Calories	.428
Protein	.4g
Carbohydrate	.63g
Sugars	.62g
Fat	.19g
Saturates	.12g

variation

When fresh peaches are out of season, canned peaches may be used instead. Thawed frozen raspberries may be used instead of fresh.

cook's tip

To peel and stone the peaches, place them in a bowl, cover with boiling water and leave for 30 seconds, then drain and plunge into a bowl of cold water. Peel off the skins, cut in half and remove the stones.

1 Preheat the oven to 150°C/300°F/Gas Mark 2. Oil a 35 x 25-cm/14 x 10-inch Swiss roll tin and line with non-stick baking paper. To make the coulis, process the raspberries and icing sugar to a purée. Press through a sieve into a bowl and reserve. To make the meringue, sift the cornflour into a bowl and stir in the sugar. In a separate, spotlessly clean bowl, whisk the egg whites into stiff peaks, then whisk in the vinegar. Gradually whisk in the cornflour and sugar mixture until stiff and glossy.

2 Spread the mixture evenly in the lined tin, leaving a 1-cm/½-inch border. Bake in the centre of the oven for 20 minutes, then reduce the heat to 110°C/225°F/Gas Mark ¼ and cook for a further 25–30 minutes, or until puffed up. Remove from the oven. Leave to cool for 15 minutes. Turn out on to baking paper.

3 To make the filling, place the peaches in a bowl with the raspberries. Add 2 tablespoons of the coulis and mix. In a separate bowl, whisk the crème fraîche and cream together until thick. Spread over the meringue. Scatter the fruit over the cream, leaving a 3-cm/1¼-inch border at one short edge. Using the baking paper, lift and roll the meringue, starting at the short edge without the border, ending up seam-side down. Lift on to a plate and serve with the coulis.

sticky coffee & walnut puddings

serves 6   **prep: 20 mins**   **cook: 30–40 mins**

These delightful little coffee puddings with a butterscotch sauce are guaranteed to delight your guests.

INGREDIENTS

55 g/2 oz butter, softened,
plus extra for greasing
1 tbsp instant coffee granules
150 g/5½ oz self-raising flour
1 tsp ground cinnamon
55 g/2 oz light muscovado sugar, sifted
2 large eggs, beaten
55 g/2 oz walnuts, finely chopped

BUTTERSCOTCH SAUCE

25 g/1 oz walnuts, roughly chopped
55 g/2 oz butter
55 g/2 oz light muscovado sugar
150 ml/5 fl oz double cream

NUTRITIONAL INFORMATION	
Calories	.520
Protein	.7g
Carbohydrate	.39g
Sugars	.21g
Fat	.38g
Saturates	.19g

cook's tip

This could be cooked as one large pudding, in which case the mixture should be put into a pudding basin, covered and steamed for 1½ hours.

1 Preheat the oven to 190°C/375°F/Gas Mark 5, then grease 6 individual metal pudding basins. Dissolve the coffee granules in 2 tablespoons of boiling water and reserve. Sift the flour and cinnamon into a bowl. Place the butter and sugar in a separate bowl and beat together until light and fluffy. Gradually beat in the eggs. Add a little flour if the mixture shows signs of curdling. Fold in half the flour and cinnamon mixture, then fold in the remaining flour and cinnamon, alternately with the coffee. Stir in the walnuts.

2 Divide the mixture between the basins. Place a piece of buttered foil over each basin and secure with an elastic band. Stand the basins in a roasting tin and pour in enough boiling water to reach halfway up the sides of the basins. Cover the roasting tin with a tent of foil, folding it under the rim.

3 Bake the puddings in the preheated oven for 30–40 minutes, or until well risen and firm to the touch.

4 Meanwhile, make the sauce. Place all of the ingredients in a saucepan over a low heat and stir until melted and blended. Bring to a simmer, then remove from the heat. Turn the puddings out on to a serving plate, spoon over the hot sauce and serve.

upside-down tropical fruit pudding

⏱ **cook: 50–60 mins**   🕐 **prep: 25 mins, plus 10 mins standing**   **serves 8**

This sticky, fruity pudding is delicious served hot with ice cream, or it can be left to cool and served as a cake.

NUTRITIONAL INFORMATION	
Calories	.472
Protein	.5g
Carbohydrate	.58g
Sugars	.41g
Fat	.26g
Saturates	.16g

INGREDIENTS

175 g/6 oz butter, softened, plus extra for greasing

175 g/6 oz light muscovado sugar

3 eggs

175 g/6 oz self-raising flour

1 tsp ground mixed spice

TOPPING

55 g/2 oz butter, softened

55 g/2 oz light muscovado sugar

2 bananas

1 small pineapple

1 mango

cook's tip

If time is limited and you want to speed up the preparation time for this recipe, the cake mixture can be mixed in a food processor.

1 Preheat the oven to 180°C/350°F/Gas Mark 4. Grease a deep 20-cm/8-inch round cake tin.

2 To make the topping, spread the butter evenly over the base of the tin and sprinkle the sugar on top. Peel the bananas and slice thickly, then peel the pineapple and mango and cut into chunks. Mix the fruit together and pile evenly over the base of the tin.

3 To make the cake, place the butter, sugar and eggs in a bowl and sift in the flour and mixed spice. Beat together until light and fluffy, then spread the mixture over the fruit. Bake in the preheated oven for 50–60 minutes, or until well risen and firm to the touch. Leave in the tin for 10 minutes, then loosen the edges with a palette knife and turn out on to a serving plate.

panettone pudding

serves 6 | **prep: 15 mins, plus 1 hr standing** | **cook: 40 mins**

This is a variation of bread and butter pudding, made with panettone, an Italian cross between bread and cake.

INGREDIENTS

40 g/1½ oz butter, softened, plus extra for greasing

250 g/9 oz panettone, cut into slices

225 ml/8 fl oz milk

225 ml/8 fl oz double cream

1 vanilla pod, split

3 eggs

115 g/4 oz golden caster sugar

2 tbsp apricot jam, warmed and sieved

NUTRITIONAL INFORMATION

Calories 496

Protein 9g

Carbohydrate 49g

Sugars 34g

Fat 31g

Saturates 17g

cook's tip

The vanilla pod used in this recipe may be rinsed clean and patted dry with kitchen paper and used again in another recipe.

1 Grease an 850-ml/1½-pint shallow ovenproof dish. Butter the slices of panettone and arrange in the dish. Place the milk, cream and vanilla pod in a saucepan over a low heat until the mixture reaches boiling point. Place the eggs and sugar in a bowl and beat together, then pour in the milk mixture and beat together.

2 Pour the custard through a sieve over the buttered panettone. Leave for 1 hour so that the panettone soaks up the custard. Preheat the oven to 160°C/325°F/Gas Mark 3.

3 Bake the pudding in the preheated oven for 40 minutes, then drizzle the apricot jam over the top. If the top crusts of the pudding are not crisp and golden, heat under a preheated hot grill for 1 minute before serving.

lemon puddle pudding

cook: 50 mins–1 hr   **prep: 15 mins**   **serves 6**

This is a hot sponge pudding, complete with its own sauce, which forms underneath the pudding while baking.

NUTRITIONAL INFORMATION

Calories 360

Protein 8g

Carbohydrate 39g

Sugars 34g

Fat 20g

Saturates 12g

INGREDIENTS

100 g/3½ oz butter, softened,

plus extra for greasing

175 g/6 oz golden caster sugar

grated rind and juice of 2 lemons

4 eggs

40 g/1½ oz plain flour

400 ml/14 fl oz milk

icing sugar, for dusting

cook's tip

Lemons vary in the amount of juice they produce, so if you think your lemons are not very juicy, use 3 in this recipe. When using the rind in a recipe, try to find unwaxed lemons.

1 Preheat the oven to 180°C/350°F/Gas Mark 4. Grease a 1-litre/1¾-pint ovenproof dish. Place the butter, sugar and lemon rind in a bowl and beat together until light and fluffy. Separate the eggs, placing the whites in a spotlessly clean bowl, and beat the yolks into the creamed butter and sugar with the flour and lemon juice.

2 Gradually stir the milk into the lemon mixture. Whisk the egg whites until stiff peaks form, then gently fold into the mixture. Pour into the prepared dish. The mixture should come halfway up the sides.

3 Stand the dish in a roasting tin and pour in enough hot water to reach a depth of 2.5 cm/1 inch. Bake in the preheated oven for 50 minutes–1 hour, or until well risen and golden. Leave to cool for 5 minutes, then dust with sifted icing sugar and serve.

ginger & lemon puddings

serves 8   **prep: 20 mins** ◔   **cook: 30–40 mins** ⏲

*These little puddings are very light and will not fill you up
too much if you serve them at the end of a heavy meal.*

INGREDIENTS

115 g/4 oz butter, softened,
plus extra for greasing

2 lemons

85 g/3 oz drained stem ginger,
chopped, plus 1 tbsp ginger syrup
from the jar

2 tbsp golden syrup

175 g/6 oz self-raising flour

2 tsp ground ginger

115 g/4 oz golden caster sugar

2 eggs, beaten

3–4 tbsp milk

vanilla custard, to serve

NUTRITIONAL INFORMATION

Calories 232

Protein 4g

Carbohydrate 24g

Sugars 8g

Fat 14g

Saturates 8g

variation

If you prefer, you can serve the
puddings with vanilla ice cream rather
than custard.

cook's tip

When grating the rind from
the lemons, be careful not to
grate any of the white pith
underneath it, otherwise the
finished dish will taste bitter.

1 Preheat the oven
to 160°C/325°F/Gas
Mark 3. Grease 8 individual
metal pudding basins. Grate
the rind from the lemons and
reserve in a bowl. Remove all
the pith from one of the
lemons and slice the flesh into
8 thin rounds. Squeeze the
juice from half of the second
lemon and reserve. Place the
ginger syrup, golden syrup and
1 teaspoon of the lemon juice
in a bowl and mix together.

2 Divide the mixture
between the prepared
pudding basins. Place a slice of
lemon in the bottom of each
basin. Sift the flour and ground
ginger into a bowl. Place the
butter and sugar in a separate
bowl and beat together until
light and fluffy. Gradually beat
in the eggs, then fold in the
flour mixture and add enough
milk to give a soft dropping
consistency. Stir in the reserved
grated lemon rind and the
chopped stem ginger.

3 Divide the mixture
between the prepared
basins. Place a piece of
buttered foil over each basin
and secure with an elastic
band. Stand the basins in
a roasting tin and pour in
enough boiling water to reach
halfway up the sides of the
basins. Cover the roasting tin
with a tent of foil, folding it
under the rim. Bake in the oven
for 30–40 minutes, or until
well risen and firm to the
touch. Turn the puddings out
on to a serving dish and serve
with vanilla custard.

apple & blackberry crumble

serves 4   **prep: 15 mins**   **cook: 40–45 mins**

A crumble is one of the easiest puddings to make and it is always a popular end to any family meal.

INGREDIENTS

900 g/2 lb cooking apples, peeled and sliced

300 g/10½ oz blackberries, fresh or frozen

55 g/2 oz light muscovado sugar

1 tsp ground cinnamon

custard or pouring cream, to serve

CRUMBLE

85 g/3 oz self-raising flour

85 g/3 oz plain wholemeal flour

115 g/4 oz butter

55 g/2 oz demerara sugar

NUTRITIONAL INFORMATION

Calories 530

Protein 6g

Carbohydrate 76g

Sugars 47g

Fat 25g

Saturates 16g

variation

Sprinkle a handful of chopped or flaked almonds over the crumble before serving, if you like.

cook's tip

When making a crumble, keep rubbing in the butter until the crumbs are quite coarse. This ensures that the crumble will be crunchy.

1 Preheat the oven to 200°C/400°F/Gas Mark 6. Peel and core the apples and cut into chunks. Place in a bowl with the blackberries, sugar and cinnamon and mix together, then transfer to an ovenproof baking dish.

2 To make the crumble, sift the self-raising flour into a bowl and stir in the wholemeal flour. Add the butter and rub in with your fingers until the mixture resembles coarse breadcrumbs. Stir in the sugar.

3 Spread the crumble over the apples and bake in the preheated oven for 40–45 minutes, or until the apples are soft and the crumble is golden brown and crisp. Serve with custard or pouring cream.

index

index

index